First published in Glasgow, 2017.

Prologue

It all started with a long, boring night shift on a cold Sunday in February. My mind was wandering in search of better, more exciting times. I glanced over a walking magazine as my machine whizzed along in the background. None of the articles really held my attention until I spotted one about a new long-distance walking route called The East Highland Way.

My wandering mind snapped to attention and I raced through the article, devouring every sentence in eager anticipation of the next. I discovered that the East Highland Way linked the Speyside Way in the north east of Scotland to the West Highland Way in the south west. After consulting my calculator I worked out that putting all three together would result in a massive long-distance walk of 238 miles in total.

As soon as my machine had finished its cycle, I walked over to my friend Frank who worked in the opposite end of the factory. I handed him the magazine, pointed to the article, and said, "Read that and tell me what you think." Then I turned and made my way back to my machine before anyone would know I was missing. A few hours later, I saw Frank's slim, six-foot-two frame walking towards me. Being a man of few words, he simply handed back the magazine and said, "What do you have in mind?"

Sixteen Months Later: Day One

Family and friends were gathered around, wishing us luck and making us pose for photos. We were uncharacteristically quiet as we contemplated the task ahead. Over a year of planning had led to this point. In front of us stretched the 238 miles of the three trails. We had set ourselves the challenge of completing the entire walk in just seven days. As the whole thing had initially been my idea, I began to feel responsible for getting the others mixed up in this madness. My stomach was churning, my mouth had all but dried up, and my confidence of the previous months was starting to feel like hollow bravado. I told myself to get a grip, focus on Day One (a 48 mile trek from Buckie to Grantown-on-Spey) and let each day take care of itself.

In my head I was shouting, "I'm not doing it and you can't make me!" Out loud, however, I tried to project an air of quiet confidence. "It's time gents," I said, letting everyone know that the time for best wishes and goodbyes was over. The five of us in the team shook hands and wished each other luck. Then, at 7:30am on Saturday the 11th of June, on a fine but overcast morning, we took the first of over a million steps for the children's charity Action for Children.

We had decided to aim for a pace of around four miles an hour. It took us a few miles to get up to speed but we soon settled into our stride. Before leaving, we had arranged to meet Uncle Jimmy, our team support, in Fochabers at around 10:30. This would be the ten mile point and a good opportunity to take in some much needed food and fluids. As we walked, the stresses of the starting point faded away and the good-humoured banter started to come through. We teased each other about everything and anything, nothing was sacred. It was clear that we were all getting our heads around what we were doing. We were knocking in the miles and whenever anyone had to stop for any reason the rest of us would keep going and let them catch up. This was unfortunate for Ally as he was stopping every fifteen minutes to pee, which meant that he must have had to run about two of the first ten miles. It seemed like every time I looked round I would see the back of Ally's stocky, balding, five-foot-eight frame assuming the peeing position. Yeeeech!

At the end of those first ten miles, we met Jimmy at a set of road works and were soon drinking hot coffee and eating flapjacks. Real athletes would have been drinking sports drinks and eating bananas. It wasn't long until we were back on our way and keeping a steady pace but within five minutes Ally had to stop again for a pee. Quick as a flash Stevie shouted, "Fuck's sake Ally, what the fuck are you doing, marking your fucking territory?" There was laughter all round. Stevie is Ally's brother and you can safely say they are far from twins. Ally is bald while Stevie has tight curly hair, Ally is quite stocky while Stevie is slim, and more to the point, they have very different personalities. They are the same height, I suppose.

As we continued along the Speyside Way, we joined a disused railway line running along the beautiful River Spey. We were making good progress as the way was well signposted and the ground here was soft underfoot. This was a blessed relief as much of the route so far had been on tarmac or rock which put pressure on our feet and joints. We talked as we walked, in a group or in pairs. Occasionally one of us would be on his own, either tagging along at the back or charging ahead in front. Frank always seemed to have someone with him, happily chatting away.

Our second meet-up point of the day was at the Highlander Inn in Craigellachie, twenty three miles into our walk. Uncle Jimmy was ready and waiting, cheery and happy to see us as always. If you put a white beard on him he would be Santa (if, of course, Santa was Glaswegian and came bearing mugs of hot coffee rather than gifts). It had just started to rain and Uncle Jimmy had found a public toilet where we could shelter, have lunch, and sort ourselves out. We gave ourselves half an hour.

This is probably a good time to explain that I am Ally's and Stevie's cousin because Uncle Jimmy is their mum's and my dad's brother. You can take some aspirin and read that again if you like. Frank found it strange at first that three middle aged men, who were by no means shrinking violets, referred to their uncle as 'Uncle' both when talking to him and about him. It wasn't long, however, before he became Frank's 'Uncle' Jimmy as well. For your sake, I will now refer to Uncle Jimmy as 'Jimmy' when possible.

To get back to the main event, we were munching away on the sandwiches, snacks, and hot coffee that Jimmy had made for us. One by one our socks and shoes were coming off and an assortment of plasters, creams, sprays, and Compeed pads were being administered. I didn't have any blisters but I did have a few hotspots that had the potential to grow into them so I put some Compeed pads on as a precaution. Everyone was bombarding Jimmy with questions: "Uncle Jimmy, have you seen my black box?"

"Uncle Jimmy, have you seen my bag?"

"Uncle Jimmy, where is the water?"

We politely took it in turns to search the van for the various items. I couldn't believe that we were already having problems with our feet after just twenty three miles. I thought we had all got it sussed. We had spent months training and experimenting with different socks, creams, and footwear. Personally, I found that if I kept it simple with my running trainers, a double layer of socks, and Vaseline, I would be fine. For carrying my kit I had a simple bum bag and a water holder hanging from my waist which could also be used to hang other items like a waterproof jacket. Ally's set-up was pretty similar and Stevie's varied from day to day. Frank had no choice but to carry a small back pack since he is diabetic and needs to carry blood-testing equipment, insulin, and a week's messages in case he needs food. Trust me, Frank can get through a lot of food.

From past experience, I knew that these challenges could throw up the unexpected. I could sense a bit of apprehension from Ally. Blisters at this early stage were not a part of his game plan. I said, "Might as well get the blisters now so we don't have to worry about them later." A bit of satire that went down like an Italian forward running into a penalty area. We drank the last of our coffee, filled our water bottles, collected some more food, and were ready to go, albeit fifteen minutes later than expected. The van looked as if a street trader was about to set up for the day. There were bags of clothing and equipment everywhere. We did start to tidy up but Jimmy told us to get going and that he would reorganise the van and have it ready for our next stop: the viaduct at the thirty five mile point.

We all found it hard to get going again. Our feet and muscles had enjoyed the rest and hadn't wanted it to come to an end so quickly. About half an hour after leaving Jimmy, Frank suddenly shouted out "A, Arsenal!" In unison, the three of us responded "What?" Frank explained the rules of the game. We would all take it in turns to pick a football team beginning with the letter "A" until one of us couldn't think of a team. That person would then gain a point, we would move on to the letter "B" and so on through the alphabet and the person with the least points at the end would win. The things you do to kill time, and to quote Thoreau, "As if you could kill time without injuring eternity." There is definitely something in that, however this time killing had a point.

As the miles ticked away, so did the letters of the alphabet. We came to the letter "R". Many teams had been mentioned, it was my turn and I was struggling to think of a team that hadn't been said. Then it came to me in a blinding flash and I couldn't believe that no one had said it before. I shouted out "Wrexham!" There were hoots of laughter and the abuse that came my way from those three bastards was well out of order.

Being dyslexic, I had an idea that I had messed up but wasn't quite sure why. Ally told me, "That starts with a 'W'". Everyone spent the rest of the game coming out with dyslexic answers. I couldn't wait for it to end. Frank called out "X" and Stevie shouted, "You should win this one Ronnie! Exeter!" Bastards!

The game seemed to fizzle out without a conclusion as we were distracted by hordes of people coming towards us. They were clumped together in small groups with gaps of anything from two to twenty minutes between them. There were men and women of all ages and fitness levels. A few of them were really struggling. That's when it dawned on me that we were in our own little 238 mile bubble. Under normal circumstances we would usually stop and talk to some of them and ask about what they were doing and why. Not on this occasion. We just nodded as we passed by and hardly even made eye contact. We had a job to do and we were focused on that and that alone. There was only room in our space for the five of us. We were now tiring and trying to work out how long it would be till we met Jimmy. His name was starting to mean much more than it once did. It was starting to mean hot coffee, food, and rest. Jimmy was starting to mean Utopia.

All of a sudden, the viaduct seemed to be upon us and our spirits lifted as we walked across the bridge over the fast-flowing River Spey. The big black van came into view and not only did it mean food, water, and rest, it meant only thirteen miles left until the end of Day One. Jimmy had the food and drink laid out for us. He had also put out any kit he thought we might need. My feet were very wet due to walking miles through wet grass. They were also very hot which had melted the glue holding my insoles in place. The insoles had bunched up underneath my arch and had been causing me quite a bit of discomfort for the last two hours. I changed my socks and trainers and for the first time in ages my feet felt dry and cosy which was a big morale booster.

This was to be the last time we saw Jimmy until the end of day one at the Grantown campsite so we discussed what he could do to make it easy for us when we got in. The only problem Jimmy would have was putting up our sleeping quarters: an enormous tent-like awning. We had organised an electric hook up which gave us the use of a kettle, microwave, and lights. I wasn't sure what time we would make the campsite, or if anything would be open to buy some hot food, so a few days earlier I had made a curry with rice and portioned it off into five throwaway containers which I then froze. I had taken it out of the freezer that morning so by the time we got to the campsite it would be just right for us to chuck in the micro.

Once we were fed, watered, and had replenished our supplies we said our goodbyes to Jimmy and started on our way. I could sense that everyone was keen to get to Grantown-on-Spey and get Day One over and done with. We'd been walking for about ten minutes when it dawned on me that I had left my waterproof jacket back at the van. I had a bit of a dilemma: should I run back and get it, and if I did, would Jimmy still be there when I got back? I decided to go for it. With my luck it would bucket down if I didn't. I ran back and luckily Jimmy was still there. I shouted, "Forgot my jacket!" grabbed it, about turned, and ran to catch the others. The old railway line didn't last for much longer. When I caught up to them, the Speyside Way signs directed us away from the river onto a fairly unworn and overgrown path (the words 'unworn' and 'overgrown' should have set alarm bells ringing: it turned out that this was an optional extra) which eventually took us to the road. We followed the road for about half a kilometre and then we were directed across an old field through some trees to a Land Rover track. Next came some muddy, dug-up bulldozer tracks which, we soon discovered, kept going back on themselves. Just what we didn't need after forty-plus miles. Things were bad enough as it was, but then we found ourselves walking in a fenced pen about eight feet wide. The farmers had obviously used the pen as a dumping ground for boulders of every shape and size from the nearby fields, and it went on forever! It was slow, precarious going. Frank was getting pretty pissed off by the situation (as were we all) and said, "I'll run ahead and give Jimmy a hand to put up the tent." There were no complaints from us.

The dirt track came to a junction with one path going forward over a fence and one path turning left up a hill. Although it was only about half past seven, it was dull and dank with a heavy atmosphere, a perfect match for our spirits at the time. We decided to climb over the fence, which in retrospect should have been our clue that this was the wrong path to choose. A short while later we found ourselves on a road which we had arrived at via another climbed fence (again, alarm bells should have been ringing!). We had long since stopped looking at the map and were just using the marked signs, which (surprise, surprise) had all but disappeared. Although we knew which road we were on, we didn't know exactly where on the road we were. We only had the official Speyside Way map, rather than an ordinance survey map that would allow us to pick up key features. We were hoping that Cromdale was behind us. Ally, holding the map, said, "Let's go this way. I think it's this way."

"Thinking isn't really good enough," I said. "We know the direction we want to be going so let's head this way to make sure."

Ally argued that if Cromdale was behind us then we would be putting two miles onto our day. My point was that at least we would know. If we went the other way we would have no idea how many miles out we were, or even if we were going in the right direction. We started walking towards the direction that we knew would eventually catch up with the Speyside Way trail. We tried to call Frank and Jimmy for an update but none of us could get a signal. After a few more minutes of walking we all jumped when my phone started to ring. I saw it was Jimmy and answered with the cheeriest, "Hello" that I could manage under the circumstances.

"I've been worried," Jimmy said. "Where are you?"

I couldn't tell him that I didn't have a clue and worry him even more so I just said, "a bit away yet, but Frank ran ahead so he should be with you soon."

"That's good. See you soon. Cheerio."

I was so pleased to have a signal. I took the opportunity to phone Frank and he confirmed that we should have gone up the hill instead of over the fence. My mood lifted slightly since I knew we were coming up to the trail and would be back on track soon, but what he said next ripped my heart out. "I'm just coming up to Cromdale," he told me. I broke the news to Ally and Stevie.

"Aye, but what does that mean?" Stevie said.

Ally answered, "Another hour and a fucking half."

There was nothing we could do, we just had to get on with it. I started my stop watch to see how far behind Frank we were. We had soon picked up the trail and as we approached Cromdale I stopped my stop watch. It read twenty two minutes, which was a relief: we hadn't lost much time, if any. Our spirits lifted somewhat, our pace quickened, and we were about two miles from Grantown when Jimmy called asking if we were okay. I asked if Frank was with him and my heart sank when he said that he wasn't. A second later he said, "No, that's him coming now." We had just crossed the Spey and were heading into forest with well-marked paths. It was around nine o'clock and because of the trees and clouds it was very dark and gloomy. We rounded a few corners and took a few turns, always hoping to see evidence of civilisation. Eventually, the yellow glow of some street lights came into view. As we passed the golf course we saw an A4 poster saying "Come on Ronnie, Frank, Stevie, and Ally, you're almost there." It was such a boost for us, a real lift. As we continued through the week, these signs turned up in different places all along the route: a wee message from my big sister Marion and her man. We were now walking beside houses and could tell from the smell in the air that there was a chip shop nearby. The smell got stronger and stronger until we were standing right next to the chipper on Grantown-on-Spey's main street. It was ten thirty and we saw that it closed at eleven. If the curry was rank then the chipper would be getting invaded. We walked through the campsite gates at ten forty-five and were greeted by Jimmy shaking his head, the erected awning, and the smell of curry. We all shook hands and gave each other hugs while talking in deep man voices. After fifteen hours and fifteen minutes, Day One was complete. The optional extra through the boulder pens and bulldozer tracks had taken our total mileage from the forty-eight we expected to the grand total of fifty-one.

Frank had already showered and was munching his way through the curry. We gave ourselves a chance to inspect our feet and complain about how sore they were. "How's your feet, big man?" I asked Frank.

His reply was not unexpected. "All right."

If I asked Frank, "How's your arm after getting mauled by that lion?" his reply would be the same. It's not that he doesn't feel pain or find it hard, he just won't tell you. For Frank, complaining won't make it better, so why bother? In the end, we got into our sleeping bags just after midnight and that's the last thing I remember about that day. How my head hit the pillow I'll never know.

Day Two: Grantown to Newtonmore (40 Miles)

The next morning I think I came to, rather than woke up, and just lay for a moment with my eyes closed waiting to see where I would feel the most pain. I slowly moved my limbs and although my back was a little stiff I felt okay. I mean, I knew I had feet, but they weren't in agony or anything. I opened my eyes to see Jimmy rolling off of his blow-up bed – not what you would call the most graceful of movements. Watching him stagger to his feet I knew instantly that he hadn't had a good night's sleep. He had the look of one of the heckler Muppets with a scrunched up face. It looked like someone had shoved a vacuum cleaner up his arse and the suction was causing his face to collapse inwards. "Sorry, was I snoring?" I said sheepishly.

"Naw! I was frozen! I thought I was gonna die!" he said with such force and feeling that I knew he wasn't joking. The thing is, our sleeping arrangements had changed from the original plan. At first, Stevie, Jimmy, and Frank were all going to sleep in the Bongo (the black van) since it was built to sleep four. Ally and I were going to sleep in the big awning. In the end, however, everyone decided to just sleep in the awning as there was plenty of room. I'm used to wild camping and have the mat and sleeping bag to suit. I've also learned to put more layers on when sleeping outside. I just had never thought to check Jimmy's kit, or anyone else's for that matter. I knew Frank's would have been fine and a quick shifty at Ally's told me his kit was better than mine. Stevie's looked okay, but Jimmy's wasn't so good. His sleeping bag was quite thin and flimsy and blow-up beds aren't bad as a put-me-up at home, but a heat-absorbing mat is best for outdoors. I offered Jimmy my sleeping bag and mat for the next night but he said he would sort it out himself. He ended up buying a better sleeping bag that he put inside the flimsy one and that seemed to do the trick.

Anyway, that morning we all climbed out of our sleeping bags very slowly. I could feel some pain in the soles of my feet now that I was standing up. "How are we feeling this morning?" I asked.

"I'm good," said Frank, without looking up from the bag he was searching through.

"Fucking sore," Stevie grunted.

"My feet are a wee bit sore but not as bad as they were in the shower last night," Ally said. "What about you?"

I was sitting down inspecting my feet. The Compeed pads I had put on as a precaution yesterday now had blisters underneath them. "Hmm. That's a first for me. Blisters after I put Compeeds on," I replied, bemused. I was stumped. I didn't know whether to take the pads off and put new ones on or just leave them as they were. I ended up putting new pads on top of the ones that were already there. I then spread Vaseline over every inch of my feet, slid my socks on, and gingerly pulled my trainers over them. Just then my phone buzzed to let me know I had a text. It was my sister Marion congratulating us on Day One and wishing us luck for Day Two. She had sent one to all of us and continued to do so every morning for the rest of the challenge.

Stevie was messing around with his boots and trainers, trying to decide which pair he was going to wear. He eventually made a decision and joined the rest of us tucking into hot, steaming porridge and coffee. I had noticed that Jimmy hadn't had any curry the night before so it was good to see him eat breakfast. Although, that probably says more about my culinary skills than it does about Jimmy's appetite.

It was a fine morning and we were talking about what we should take with us and how long it would take to get to the first stop of the day: Boat of Garten railway station. Jimmy told us that he would sort out the tent since it was easy enough to take down. He also gave us a lift to the starting point to avoid adding any extra distance to our day. In return, we gave him the runaround. Since Frank had taken a different road into Grantown than we did, we were all giving Jimmy different directions. After many three-point turns, and a bit of arguing, we were out of the van and saying our goodbyes to Jimmy. We stood in silence and watched the Bongo disappear round the corner.

For the first few miles of walking we didn't speak too much. Probably because our feet were stinging and we were a bit concerned about how the day would pan out. After a while though, our feet seemed to improve. I'm not sure why. Maybe your body gets used to the pain, or the pressure of your steps triggers something that eases the pain, who knows! After crossing an old bridge over the River Spey we walked beside the river along quite a flat and well-defined path. The sun was shining through the clouds and the intermittent treeline meant that we were walking between shade and sunshine. We were setting quite a good pace and chatting about the sponsorship money we were raising; what Hilary – the fundraiser for Action for Children – had been doing to help us; and how Jimmy was playing a blinder for us. When I first asked Jimmy if he would be our support I tried to explain that his role was key and if he messed up then the challenge would be in doubt (no pressure there, then). He had approached the whole thing quite casually and I didn't think he really realised what we were doing or how important his part in it would be. As the start date drew closer, however, I think it began to sink in, and hats off to him, he put everything into it; which was good, because we needed him to.

It seemed like no time at all before we arrived at Nethy Bridge. It was just after nine o'clock and we were all warming up as the sun's rays shone down on us. As soon as we entered the village, we turned right and crossed an old stone hump bridge. We walked past a row of council-type houses and then were diverted away from the B-road by a Speyside Way marker onto a dirt track that ran parallel to the road about twelve feet away. Both the road and path ran through quite a thick forest. We ambled along nicely until the path joined the road, then we followed the road until it forked off and had a sign pointing in either direction. Neither one was pointing to anywhere we wanted to be. We realised right away that we had missed a signpost and, after a few choice words from each of us, we about turned and went back the way we had come.

We walked along, searching with fixed stares for a signpost or path that led through the trees. As we rounded a slight bend, a jolly-hockey-sticks type appeared with her black lab. She had long, greying hair under a wide-brimmed cowboy hat, which was tilted so that just one eye was shaded. I couldn't see any obvious signs of makeup (which she didn't need anyway). She wore a crisp white shirt, tan slacks, an embroidered green waistcoat, and tan Doctor Marten-type ankle boots. Nothing seemed to go together, but in a strange sort of way, it worked. As soon as we saw her everyone called out, "Is the Speyside Way this way?" The poor woman jumped out of her skin, but she soon realised that, although we were quite desperate, we were harmless. She half laughed, half smiled, and pointed back the way she had come. "Just up there," she said, in the most proper and posh English accent. Not only did she look the part, she had a voice to match. "Up there" turned out to be near Nethy Bridge. We had added on a diversion of one and a half miles. Once we realised where we had gone wrong, we could instantly see why. The signpost was mostly hidden by some overgrown bushes, so it was no surprise that we missed it. We were so happy to be back on the right track and to have a break from the tarmac road which had been so painful on our feet. Soon enough, we heard the whistle of an old-fashioned steam train. Boat of Garten railway station – our first stop of the day – was just minutes away.

When we arrived at the station we could see the beautiful steam engine sending fluffy clouds of smoke rising up into the clear blue sky. Outside the station there was a set of three benches arranged in a u-shape, a small car park where the Bongo was parked, and a few shops.

Jimmy was sitting on one of the benches enjoying the warmth of the sun. He had clearly been catching up on some of the sleep he had lost the night before. As had become the custom, he shook hands with us one by one. As everyone else picked their way through the food that Jimmy had got for us, I went to one of the shops to try to buy a pair of insoles since mine were still scrunching up. I returned empty-handed, however, and the only sandwich left was ham salad. By the time I picked off the tomato and cucumber and scraped off the pink runny stuff it was a ham sandwich with a bit of lettuce. We all took our shoes off, giving our sore bits as much of a break as we could, and settled down into a pleasant half hour of chatting and relaxing in the sun. Jimmy told us that some people had helped him take down the tent as he had had some difficulties with it. I told him that we would make sure it was packed away before we left in future. Our next stop would be Aviemore, marking the end of the Speyside Way and the beginning of the East Highland Way. Since the latter was a new long-distance walk, it had no marker posts. It also had some optional extras which, in the end, we decided to miss out and just go the most direct route since we had already done about four and a half miles more than we should have.

Shoes and socks were gingerly put on and we all winced as the burning, stinging, aching pain in our feet came back as soon as we stood up. We groaned and laughed nervously as we shook Jimmy's hand and said our goodbyes. As we walked, the pain eased, and we entertained ourselves by quoting lines from Gregory's Girl (one of our favourite films), telling jokes and re-enacting sketches from shows like Still Game and Chewin' the Fat. Stuff we had all heard a thousand times before but still made us giggle like school boys. There was a pause in the conversation and we were all walking along, happily caught up in our own thoughts, when, out of the blue, Frank shouted out, "A! ABBA!"

"Adam and the Ants!" Ally responded.

Stevie went next with ABC, and then they all turned to look at me. They were grinning like demented madmen in an asylum, waiting for their medication, willing me to give them a dyslexic answer. Truth be told, if I could've thought of one, I would have. Instead, I said, "Aztec Camera" and it was game on. There was really only ever going to be one winner in this game though. Frank is the music man. The rest of us did our best but we just weren't in the same league. Ally and I were pretty much neck-and-neck, but Stevie was diabolical and definitely got most of the teasing this time around.

As we came into Aviemore Stevie had started to slow up a bit and lag behind, so when we came to a split in the path we waited for him to make sure he took the correct route. He wasn't too far back but when he did catch up his unusual silence and his body language said it all. His first stop was to get more Compeed pads and painkillers. That said, everyone's feet were giving them problems. I went to the walking shop to see if I could manage to get some insoles this time. The only ones I could see were priced at £34. "Do you have any other insoles, cheaper ones, maybe?" I said to the assistant, more pleading than asking.

"No, that's it I'm afraid, but they do have a money-back guarantee if you're not satisfied. Just send us the receipt and the insoles," he said in his best professional tone.

"Okay, can you fit them for me? I don't have anything to cut them with," I sighed.

"No problem."

"There will be a problem as soon as I take my trainers off and you get a whiff of my feet, you robbing bastard," I said. Inwardly. To myself. Normally I would have been embarrassed and self-conscious at removing my trainers because I knew how bad the odour was going to be. Today, however, I eased them off with great gusto and handed them to the assistant with a wry smile that pretty much said, "Get a whiff of that, Dick Turpin." I wiggled my toes as I strolled around the shop, releasing as much cheesy odour from my very damp, crusty socks as possible. I stood next to as many fellow customers as I could while doing my best to waft my sweaty body odour. If I could have just squeezed out a curry fart I could have cleared the shop and cost them a fortune. If I sound bitter and twisted, it's because I was! Thirty-four quid for a pair of insoles! Money-back guarantees my arse. Soon enough, the assistant handed me my shoes, trying hard not to show his disgust. I put them on and left the shop clutching my receipt, which I would definitely be sending back to get my no-quibble refund. They didn't even feel different to any other insoles I'd tried. For £34 I should have been walking on fluffy clouds of nothingness!

I went to meet the others at the end of the Speyside Way. To this day, I haven't told them how much the insoles cost – I just did not want the ribbing. We celebrated the end of the first leg, savouring the moment. We were really chuffed to get all sixty-six-plus miles completed in just one and a half days. After taking a few photos and congratulating each other, the Speyside Way guide book was put away and the Ordinance Survey map which covered the East Highland Way was put in my waterproof map case. It wouldn't leave my side until the end.

As we were walking through the shops and cafés on Aviemore Main Street, the smell of chip-shop chips suddenly hit my nostrils, causing my mouth to water instantly. The craving for hot, crispy, salt and vinegar soaked chips was still there from the night before. I followed my nose and came out of the chip shop with a very large bag of chips and a can of coke (what did I say about an athlete's diet again?). I don't think I've ever enjoyed a bag of chips so much. To top it off, I had just put the empty bag in the bin when Ally handed me an ice cream cone. All that yumminess was such a boost that I even forgot about the £34 insoles.

About four miles into the East Highland Way the tarmac started causing us all problems, especially Stevie. He was starting to hobble rather than walk and was lagging behind again. He was in pain and not hiding it very well. We stopped for a rest to see if we could help him but he was adamant that he would just wait until we got to Insh, our next stop. We had just started to get going again when there was the sound of what seemed to be a sizeable pipe band in the distance. We stopped and stared at each other. Frank said, "Is that a –"

"– pipe band," Ally interrupted.

"Cannae be," I said.

"We're in the middle of nowhere," said Stevie.

We stood for a moment in silence to try and work out which direction it was coming from but the sound just disappeared. We shrugged and continued on our way. The tarmac was causing us serious problems by this point. Then the sound of the pipe band started up again, but it was closer this time. We stopped in our tracks as the skirl of the pipes grew louder and louder by the minute. All was revealed when the Bongo came flying round the corner. The windows were down and we could see Jimmy's strong, hairy arm doing the queen's wave out the driver's window. The sound of the pipes and drums were coming from his CD player. As he got closer the tune became recognizable and we all cheered as he passed by with 'Scotland the Brave' blaring from the speakers. A moment later, he was gone, the Bongo disappearing over a slight bump in the road, with Jimmy's arm still waving out of the window. It was such a surreal moment that we all burst out laughing. Our spirits lifted, and we got on our way again, talking and laughing about what had just happened. When we got to Insh, Jimmy had laid out food, water, and coffee on a table. The medical bag and all of our personal items were at hand in the Bongo. For Ally, Stevie, and me, the medical bag took priority over everything else. Frank went straight for the food and fluid but the rest of us followed our now familiar routine of sitting down and taking our socks and shoes off to inspect our feet.

I had Compeed pads on the balls and inside heels of both feet. The balls of my feet were sore, but I couldn't make out if I had blisters. The heels, on the other hand, had blisters that were obvious even through two sets of Compeeds. I decided not to change anything for the moment and to wait until the end of the day before doing anything about them. I took two paracetamol and two ibuprofen and made note of the time so that I could take the same dose in four hours. I've always hated taking anti-inflammatories as they sometimes cause me to have bad asthma attacks. For the rest of the challenge, the tablets and my asthma inhaler were never far from my side. Stevie and Ally had also made changes to their dressings and taken an array of painkillers and we were soon munching our way through sandwiches and drinking coffee. We talked about how weird it felt that it was only Sunday. It seemed as though it should be nearer Wednesday with the amount we'd done so far. Time seemed to have stopped, and in place of the minutes and hours were yards and miles.

Stevie decided to get going early as he was conscious of holding us up. We let him go and gave Jimmy a hand to pack the Bongo. We now knew that after we rested we would be in excruciating pain for the first mile or so. Somehow we'd just accepted that that's the way it was, and we even managed to rip the piss out of each other for walking like monkeys. It took us about an hour to catch up with Stevie. He was limping heavily but still managing a good pace. We made it to Kingussie barracks just after 6pm. Although they were in ruins, the barracks were an impressive sight, sitting on what looked like a sizeable man-made hill. They had been built for the redcoats after the Jacobite uprising of 1745. That period in Scottish history for me is so fascinating and romantically tragic that it could never be surpassed by any other story – fact or fiction. We were all tiring now and eager for Day Two to be over and resigned to our own bit of history. There wasn't much chat as our spirits, as well as our bodies, were flagging. Stevie was a bit behind, with Frank walking with him to make sure he was okay. Not too much later, we entered Newtonmore, an old Victorian village with a long main street lined with granite buildings.

Ally phoned Jimmy to tell him to pick us up at the next day start point, which was at the end of the village. Jimmy told us that he binned the original campsite and got us into one about four miles closer. Ally went into what looked like the last pub in the village to see what time they stopped serving food. Thankfully, this turned out to be 9pm. It was around 8pm at this point so we headed straight to the campsite to get ready. When we arrived, we discovered that the campsite was nothing like the one we had stayed in the night before in Grantown. That campsite had been equipped with heated toilet and shower blocks which were tastefully decorated with simple plain tiles, large smoked mirrors, and soft music playing in the background. This campsite was an enormous field with a concrete shack at one end that was barely watertight and definitely not windproof. The shower cubicles were made of brick and cost 20p to use. The toilet cubicle had an old shed door on it. The shack also had a room with a washing machine and a couple of electric plugs that were also 20p to use. Under normal circumstances I would have called it a dump, a midden, a shithole. But these were not normal circumstances and after walking over ninety miles in two days, this was the Ritz. Frank and I put up the big tent while Stevie and Ally showered. There was no way Stevie could have helped out and the fact that Ally left it to Frank and me made it clear that Ally was struggling too. That's not to say that Frank and I were in any great shape, but we had been at this point on previous challenges so it wasn't quite the same shock to the system that Ally and Stevie were experiencing. Once the tent was up, the mats, sleeping bags and extra clothes were laid out. Showered, changed, and full of painkillers, we made our way to the pub for a well-deserved hot meal and a couple of pints.

We ordered our drinks and sat at the table to wait for the food to arrive. It gave us a chance to assess how things were going so far. Jimmy told us that he had found the first couple of days quite intense and that it hadn't been quite what he expected. Stevie was looking quite pale and kept disappearing to the toilet. When the food arrived, it looked amazing. I felt absolutely famished and got tucked in to my steak pie. After only a few mouthfuls, however, I felt very full. Everyone else pretty much scoffed theirs but I just picked my way around the plate, eating very little. We ordered another round of drinks but I only managed to get through half of my pint. Stevie was looking quite ill at this stage and went to the toilet to be sick a couple of times. I think that having the chance to sit down and relax had only made the fatigue hit us even harder. We went back to the campsite, brushed our teeth, and curled up in our sleeping bags. We were just nodding off when Frank let go a ripper of a fart. We all burst out laughing like school boys, and that's pretty much the last memory I have of that day.

Day Three: Newtonmore to Spean Bridge (43 Miles)

I blinked open my eyes and tried to get to grips with where I was. Looking up, all I could see was the blue roof of the tent, but I could visualise the weather above it easily enough. The rain was making a continual rat-tat-tat sound and the entire tent was moving back and forward with the wind. I turned over, sank my entire body into my sleeping bag, pulled the drawcord tight over my head and started slipping back into unconsciousness. The noise of the wind and rain faded into the background, but they were soon replaced by an even more obnoxious sound. I was on the edge of drifting back to sleep when my phone buzzed, startling me awake again. It was 6am and time to get up. Like moths from cocoons we reluctantly slunk out from the confines of our snug sleeping bags. There was a collective groan as our bodies shifted from warm, cosy, sleepy mode to cold, yucky, reality mode.

Apart from my feet, I felt okay. I didn't stand up, just swung my legs around to examine my sore bits. I glanced around to see the others doing the same. Looking at Jimmy, I could tell he was concerned. His mood and his body language told me that he wasn't feeling confident. "I'll put the kettle on," he said, and left the tent. The mood in general was sombre as we started looking through our medical bags for painkillers, pads, creams, etc. I took what was becoming my usual mixture of ibuprofen and paracetamol and made a mental note that it would be 10am before my next fix. Once that was done, there was nothing else for it but to peel off my socks and take a look at my feet.

It turned out that there were almost identical problems on both feet. The right was more damaged than the left, but the bruising and blisters were in the same places. I tried to pull the Compeed pads off the inside of my left heel, but every time I pulled, the pain shot up my leg as the blister started to tear. I had another go at it, this time holding the blistered skin down while pulling the pad off. Bit by bit I managed to edge the pad away from my skin to show an un-burst blister of about an inch and a half in diameter. The fluid underneath stretched my skin out like a water balloon. "I'll leave that there for now," I thought, and concentrated on the pads on the ball of my foot. There was no sign of a blister, but I could feel the bruising. I tried to lift the pad but the pain was unbearable. "Okay, one quick movement," I thought, easing the pads just enough to get a grip of them with my thumb and forefinger. I took a few deep breaths, counted, "One, two, three..." and pulled with all my might. Pain shot through my entire body. I sat there, eyes closed, body rigid, waiting for the pain to ease. All my other senses gave way to the sense of touch, which was telling me that I shouldn't have touched that fucking Compeed pad. After what seemed like an eternity, the pain slowly ebbed away to a dull throb. I slowly opened my eyes, unsure of what I might see. It was worse than I could have imagined. Three quarters of the pad was in my hand...and the other quarter was still stuck to my foot. When Compeed pads stick, they stick fast. "Fuck that," I thought. The bit that was left stuck to my foot could wait. There was no way I was putting myself through that again today.

The ball of my foot was not cut or blistered and there were no obvious signs of damage, but believe you me, it was throbbing. I looked up to check on the others and it was like a scene from Michael Jackson's "Thriller", the way they were all groaning and jerking about. Ally was having the same problem as me: trying to remove a Compeed pad from the ball of his foot. After much grunting and groaning he took a deep breath and said, with a sense of relief, "Fuck that," and left the pad on. He smeared Vaseline on his feet and put his socks on. Frank looked like he was trying to stare-out the sole of his foot with one eye, while biting his lip. I have no idea what he was trying to do. Stevie was looking grey and had bits of cloth and plasters stuck all over his toes and feet. I decided to take a look at my right foot.

The Compeed pad on the ball of my foot looked like it had been swallowed up by the skin and flesh surrounding it, and the ones on my heel looked like a bulging red light bulb. I started to pull at the pad on the ball of my foot and managed to prise it off with some discomfort but nothing like the pain of my left foot. I looked at the ones on my heel and thought, "This is going to be really sore." I gave it a very small tug...and the whole thing moved! "Result," I said to myself and gave another gentle pull. Amazingly, the two pads fell off with considerable ease and very little pain. Unfortunately, the skin and flesh underneath fell off with them. Bright red blood spilled over my heel and dripped onto the dark green of my sleeping mat. Ally gave a nervous laugh and said, "Look, Ronnie's a leper." Frank and Stevie looked over but didn't say a word. They had problems of their own to contend with.

I grabbed the sock I had just taken off and pressed it to my heel with one hand. With my free hand I searched through the medical bag and pulled out some sterile wipes, Vaseline, and plasters. I took the sock away from the wound, hoping that the bleeding would have stopped, but as soon as I moved it, the bright red blood sprung up and spilled over my heel once more. I sat for a while, pressing the sock hard on the wound. When the bleeding finally slowed I wiped it with a sterile wipe until I was satisfied that it was clean. Then I put a big dollop of Vaseline on the sore and a plaster on top. Next, I burst the blister on my other heel and went through the same process. The last stage was dressing the balls of my feet. Once all that was done, I put my shorts and vest top on and threw my waterproof trousers and jacket on top. I sat down and eased my socks on, trying not to dislodge any of the dressings, and then put my trainers over the top, which was actually much easier than I thought it would be. Although I was a bit sore and uncomfortable, I was at least pleased that the Compeed pads were off as I think they had been starting to cause more problems than they solved.

I went to join Jimmy and he handed me a cup of steaming hot coffee. The smell of the rich coffee beans was comforting as I looked out on the cold, wet, miserable day. I wrapped both hands around the cup and took a sip. At that moment in time that sip of coffee was just about the best thing in the world. "Are you okay?" Jimmy asked, "Will you manage to walk?"

"I have an open wound on my heel, but I'll be okay," I replied, as matter-of-factly as I could. I knew that today was make-or-break day. Not just for me, but for the others as well.

Jimmy dropped us off and we each shook his hand and said our goodbyes. We then stood in silence as we watched Jimmy and the Bongo disappear around the slight bend. We didn't move, just listened as the noise of the engine faded away. It was almost completely gone when Frank hit out with, "I always said that Uncle Jimmy was round the bend." We all burst out laughing. The joke was so perfectly timed. We sprung back to life with our mood lifted and went on our way coming out with one-liners, ripping each other to shreds, and telling funny stories.

We made our way up a steep tarmac lane with very posh houses on either side. All at once, the houses stopped, and we were in open countryside with glens below us and hills all around. The tarmac lane ended at a sizeable car park where we then joined a dirt path leading downhill towards a little wooden bridge. The bridge passed over a small burn which ran into the river about a quarter of a mile away. We squelched our way down the muddy path towards the river, ankle deep in muddy, grass-filled bog. We decided to make our way to the slightly higher ground to our right, hoping that it would be less boggy, which of course it wasn't. However, the higher ground gave us a good vantage point so that we could see both the bothy and the path that we had to get to. Unfortunately, we could also see the shallow, but very fast-flowing, river (courtesy of the endless rain) and the mile and a half of bog that we had to cross to get to the bothy. There are some things you're better off not knowing.

There was a path that we could have followed but due to the constant rain it had turned into a small, rock-filled stream. Since we were already as wet as we were going to get, we really had nothing to lose. We stood for a moment at the river bank, then I said, "Fuck it! Let's do it," and walked knee deep into the shallow river. I made it across to the other side, where things only got worse. The ground was so boggy it was like walking through treacle. On every step my feet were held down with the suction created by the mixture of mud, water, and moss. We were all walking in slow motion, and it was made even more difficult by the way that the bog went up and down in twenty-five to thirty metre dips and rises. We'd focus on our goal (the bothy) but then go down into a dip so that the bothy was out of sight and unknowingly start veering off to the left or right, only discovering our mistake when we came to another rise in the ground. This hellish nightmare lasted for about an hour until we finally reached the bothy. I sat inside to turn my map to the correct page and then we headed downhill. There was a good path there which felt like carpet after our hour's trek in the treacle.

About ten minutes after leaving the bothy I started feeling burning electric shock-type pain going up my shin and into my right knee. I knew instantly what it was. "Fucking shin splints," I thought angrily. I've suffered with this problem before and there's no way of getting rid of them. I turned to tell Ally and Stevie my tale of woe but noticed that Stevie was having a really difficult time and didn't need to share mine as well. Frank was well ahead, but we caught up with him for a bit when he stopped at a split in the path to make sure he was going the right way. In hindsight I should have given him the map. We eventually got onto the road that led to Laggan where we would meet Jimmy for rest, hot drinks, and some food. Frank was up ahead again by this point, Ally and I were about five minutes behind him, and Stevie was really toiling. He was hobbling quite badly and, as we waited every now and then to let him catch up, I began to have my first doubts about him finishing the day, never mind the next four.

When we got to Laggan we enjoyed our rest and intake of food and fluids, but had to get going quick enough since we were well behind schedule and cooling down fast in the wind and rain. We got going again and were chatting away like fishwives when Stevie announced that a few weeks earlier he had secretly emailed all of our wives asking questions about our married lives. His plan was to do a "Mr and Mrs Quiz" with the winner getting a prize. Our gasps of horror seemed to surprise him, and he was quite taken aback with the amount of abuse that came his way. I started the onslaught, saying, "Are you off your fucking head you stupid Swede fuck! Aye, the winner is covered in glory but the losers will have a life-long nagging to look forward to."

Frank weighed in next, "I don't know about Swedish women, but Scottish women don't need any ammunition without you loading the gun."

Ally stopped walking and just looked at Stevie and shook his head before asking, "Did your mum drop you on your head as a baby?"

Of course, we weren't really angry with Stevie (even though as ideas go it was up there with the Captain of the Titanic deciding to have a closer look at the icebergs). He just gave us an opportunity to give him a whole lot of grief and we took good advantage of that for the next two hours. It took his mind off the pain at least. A mile or two further on and Stevie was all but waving the white flag, but we could smell blood and were going in for the kill. Luckily for him, at that moment we came across a café and a large car park that marked the end of the cycle path. A café also meant a toilet and Frank announced that he had a steamer he'd been holding on to all morning and he would need to use the facilities. Stevie said that since he was here, he would go as well. The toilet was locked so they went to get the key from the café. Since the toilet was for customers only they also came out with four of the most revolting coffees I've ever tasted. They went hobbling up to the toilets and Ally and I both laughed at the way they were both clearly struggling in very different ways. Stevie's was a wide-stance hobble due to his sore feet, while Frank's was a legs-tight-together, Charlie Chaplin style hobble due to the turtle's head hanging out of his arse.

It took us an absolute age to get to the north-eastern side of Loch Laggan. By now Stevie was in quite a lot of pain and was really slowing up which meant that the chance of ending the day's walk before midnight was becoming very slim. We were walking headlong into a freezing wind that continuously threw rain straight into our faces. Ally and I were a couple of minutes ahead of Stevie and Frank so we stopped at the castle where 'Monarch of the Glen' was filmed and took some photos. Since Frank has poor circulation due to his diabetes, the slow pace meant that he was cooling down very quickly. He nodded at Stevie and said, "Who's going to take a shot of walking with the hobbit?" There were laughs all round, especially from Stevie. Ally and I slowed to walk with him and Frank charged on to go and meet Jimmy. The rest of the walk along the loch was horrendous. Stevie got slower and slower by the mile, which was frustrating for all of us. There was no laughter, no games, and no story-telling. We just ambled along and watched as Stevie winced in agony. The only time there was anything close to banter was when Stevie stopped to put Vaseline on his bum to try and stop the chafing and we tried to take a photo of him applying it. We were tired, sore, and emotional. So little progress had been made over the past four hours that it was approaching 6pm by the time we saw the Bongo in the gloomy distance, and we still had fifteen miles to go to finish the day. As we approached the Bongo, Stevie said, "That's it. I'm finished!" No one argued or protested, I think we had all known that this would be the case after Laggan. Frank and Jimmy came out of the van and walked towards us. "I've made an executive decision," Jimmy said, "We're abandoning the campsite and staying at a hotel in Fort William. I got Jackie to book it." (Jackie being Jimmy's affluent daughter and my little cousin). I thought, "Good decision, but God, how much is this going to cost?" but I just said, "Stevie's finished. Let's get grubbed up, watered, and finish this."

Frank put his face in mine and said forcefully, "We won't make Spean Bridge tonight."

I replied just as forcefully, "You might fucking not, but I will."

Our good-humoured banter was well and truly out the window. Pain, fatigue, and frustration had taken over. We started nudging each other to get into the van for equipment. Coffee was being spilled and left with no apologies given. Frank, Ally, and I were all arguing about what to do next. Everyone was talking but no one was listening. Jimmy stood to one side and said, with arms out-stretched, "Am I allowed an opinion?" We stopped arguing and listened to him. "Why don't you walk for as long as you can and then call me and I'll come and get you? That way you'll be able to carry on tomorrow rather than kill yourselves tonight getting to Spean Bridge."

These were wise words, and of course he was one hundred percent correct, but I was really struggling with the thought of not finishing the day. I nodded reluctantly in agreement as deep down I knew he was right. Everyone quieted down and we had some food and drink. Not long later, Ally stood up and said, "Okay guys, let's go."

I started getting my stuff together and then turned around to see Stevie with his boots on, getting ready to come with us. I couldn't hide my surprise and blurted out, "What the fuck are you doing?"

"Getting ready to move out."

I really didn't know whether to punch him or hug him. He'd made the right decision half an hour ago when he chose to give it up. He'd been in agony all day, his feet were a mess, and he was causing the rest of us problems because we were making little progress. On the other hand, he didn't want to give up even though he knew all that lay ahead of him was pain, fatigue, and a mental struggle to keep going. I must admit that I had a lump in my throat as I looked at him. If he felt as bad as he looked he was in a shit state. I wanted to say something to him, to give him some encouragement, but the lump in my throat was stopping me. If I spoke I knew that my voice would quiver and my emotions would get the better of me, so I simply put my arm around his shoulder, gave him a quick squeeze, and nodded. Then I walked away so that the others wouldn't see my glazed eyes.

When we got started again we all took it in turns to walk with Stevie and tried to keep him focused and talk about anything that might take his mind off of the miles that lay ahead. "Never mind, we'll have a comfy bed tonight," I said, trying to cheer him up.

"Good stuff, what did Jimmy book?" he replied.

"I'm not sure, Jacqueline booked it," I said. I could tell by the look on his face that the pain went straight from his feet to his wallet.

"Oh," was his only reply.

For about half an hour Ally walked with him, doing the big brother bit. Then Frank walked with him and talked about all the sports they liked and the runs they wanted to do in the future. After a bit, Ally and I stopped and waited for them to catch up. Ally was getting really concerned by this point. We all were to be honest. "Okay mate, that's it for the day," we said once he'd caught up, but he was adamant that he was carrying on. For the next hour or so I stayed at the back with him and talked about his wife and kids. He was all over the place by now. His head was wobbling, arms hanging, and he was staggering like a drunk. I was just about to pull the plug for him when he stopped, put his hand on my shoulder, and said in a whisper, "Call Uncle Jimmy to pick us up."

I was so relieved when those words came out of his mouth. It had been starting to get dangerous, but I wanted it to be his decision to stop. Stevie is very fit and his legs and body were fine, but walking for forty-plus miles a day in increasing agony just drains you physically and mentally. When he finally called it quits we were only six miles from Spean Bridge! No one could deny that Stevie had given it everything he had. I tried to phone Jimmy but had no signal. "Stay where you are," I told Stevie, "I'll run on and catch the others and see if they have a signal." I ran for about five minutes but had to stop and start walking. It wasn't long before I saw Ally and Frank sitting on a wall at the side of the road. A bit out of breath, I said, "Stevie is fucked. He wants us to phone Jimmy."

"It's done," Frank replied, "He's on his way. We gathered that was the case."

I waited with them and by the time Jimmy came Stevie was walking towards us. Ally looked at him, shook his head, and said, "He needs slapped." From the way he said it I could tell that he was proud of how his wee brother kept going.

We arrived at the hotel at around 10:30pm. It turned out to be okay, nothing too fancy. Something any one of us would have booked. Why did we ever doubt Jacqueline? She's a Glasgow girl, my Uncle Jimmy's daughter, and very grounded. Come to think of it, I can't ever remember her mentioning money to me.

Hats off to Jimmy once more, he had emptied the van on his own and had already put all of our stuff in the rooms which meant we could just have a quick shower and grab something to eat. We ordered our food at a nearby chip shop but while we were waiting I felt really ill and had to go outside to throw up. Then, as soon as I had a bit of my haggis I felt instantly full. I forced the rest of it down and gave my chips to the rest of the guys to devour. Once they'd finished those we went back to the rooms. Ally and Stevie were sharing one room, and Frank, Jimmy, and I had the other. Jimmy was soon in his bed and Frank and I had a glass of red wine and chatted for fifteen minutes. We slid into our comfortable beds just after midnight. One again, I can't even remember my head hitting the pillow.

Day Four: Spean Bridge to Kinlochleven (26 Miles)

I woke up feeling like someone was forcing red hot, size three stilettos on my feet. I checked my watch and saw that it was only 4:30am. After sitting up and taking my fix of painkillers like some drug-crazed addict, I hobbled off to the bathroom, using the wall to support me. I sat on the loo and looked down at my feet. The open wound on my heel was looking okay, but the rest of my feet were bright red and swollen. I also noticed that there was a deep split in my skin on my right foot, between the big toe and the one next to it. When I lifted my foot to have a closer look I found that it ran from between my toes to about an inch into the ball of my foot. It was the weirdest thing. There was no blood or fluid leaking from it, just a deep gap in my skin. At that moment I thought it was all over for me and I went into a blind panic.

I ran the bath slowly with cold water, trying not to disturb Jimmy and Frank. I filled it just enough to cover my feet, then sat on the edge of the bath and slowly lowered my feet into the icy water. I half expected to see clouds of steam coming up as my very hot feet hit the ice cold water. The relief was almost instant. For the next couple of hours I sat there with my elbows on my knees and my hands under my chin and dozed off, every now and then waking with a jolt when my head slipped from my hand. Sometime after 5am Jimmy opened the toilet door and was taken aback to see me sitting with my feet in the bath. He stared for a moment, shook his head, had a pee, and left. Not long after that the 6am alarm started to sound and I reluctantly took my feet out of the water. They looked and felt far better and I was confident that I would be able to walk.

Frank and I spent some time fixing our feet and were almost ready to go when Ally came in looking rather sullen. "Stevie's not going to manage – he's in tears," he said, whispering. The four of us stood looking at each other, and a minute later Stevie hobbled into the room. He sat on the edge of the bed, looked at the floor, and tried to hold back the tears. "I'm sorry," he said, "I can't do it. I can't walk anymore." Then he put his hands up to his face and started to cry. We were gutted for him, but we knew he couldn't have done anymore. He had nothing else to give.

I put my arm around him and said, "You've just been unlucky mate."

"It could have been any one of us, Stevie," said Frank.

All of which Ally had probably said to him in their room. It was cold comfort. The bottom line was that after all the hard work, preparation, planning, and a week away from his family in Sweden, it was all over for him. He was understandably totally distraught. It didn't seem right to go without him, but we had to do it. We were just about to go get the last of our things together when, God bless him, Stevie stood up and said through the tears, "I'll give Uncle Jimmy a hand and make sure the rest of you finish it." He could have done many things. He could have taken the first train back to Glasgow and said that was it over for him. The fact that he still wanted to do his bit for the team speaks volumes about his character. I have always thought well of him, but my admiration for that man Stevie Paul grew enormously after that. In all honesty, I hadn't fully appreciated how important or demanding Jimmy's role was going to be. The extra pair of hands would be a great help for him, and ultimately, for the team.

Jimmy paid for the rooms and wouldn't take any money from us. If truth be told, we didn't put up much of a fight. It wasn't that we didn't want to pay our way, it's just that when Jimmy puts his mind to something he won't budge. We loaded the gear into the van and had our breakfast cereal standing in the car park. It was a slightly overcast morning, but pleasantly warm. Frank had taken a look at the East Highland Way guidebook the night before and he pointed out that if we started back about a mile from where we had finished for the night, we could take a different route which would let us avoid the tarmac road. It would put extra distance on our day, but it would be worth it to give our feet a rest from the hard, unrelenting tarmac.

We were all very quiet in the van as we travelled to the starting point. When we got there we did the usual handshake thing and said very solemnly, "See you in Fort William." As I watched the van fade into the distant, Ally gave me a playful punch in my upper arm and said, "C'mon." It was horrible leaving Stevie behind and the hijinks and good-humoured banter were well and truly gone by this point. The dynamic had completely changed and we only really talked when we had to. It started to get quite hot as the day went on. We were all in pain of varying degrees and our spirits were very low. Although Frank wouldn't complain about his pain, Ally and I were happy to tell the world how sore we were. We were all missing Stevie. He's the cheekiest wee bastard in the world and always wants to rip the piss out of someone. I don't think any of us realised or appreciated just how much he brought to the group until he was gone. We were so demotivated and out of it that when a woman came riding over to us in some sort of beach buggy thing and said, "If you go that way, you'll end up in the river," we just said, "Ta." and turned around. There was no double checking, ripping the piss, or arguing. Even though it was the shortest day in terms of miles, I knew that it was going to feel endless if things carried on the way they were going.

We got back onto the A82 just after Altour and walked along the grass verge. The road was really busy and the traffic flew by at high speed, blowing dust and small stones at us. After a kilometre we joined a path that led us in between the road and Leanachan Forest for around six kilometres before going over a slight hill. As we came over the brow of the hill we saw Fort William and the massive bulk of Ben Nevis in the distance, which gave us all a wee bit of a lift. Our pace quickened and the terrain changed from countryside to pockets of houses and warehouses. We eventually came out onto a main road next to Ben Nevis and walked uphill on the very wide and quiet tarmac. The sun was bright and there wasn't a cloud in the sky. As we continued along the road we came to the Ben Nevis Ski Centre, which I knew meant that we had gone wrong somewhere. I studied the map and discovered that we hadn't veered too far off track, and that there was a Land Rover track just up ahead that would take us back onto the main road. Once we got there, we had a choice of going over a narrow bridge or turning left before it. We turned left and after about twenty minutes arrived at a car park which marked the ascent up the north side of Ben Nevis. As we were used to doing by now, we turned around, and went over the narrow bridge we should have gone over twenty minutes earlier. This brought us onto the road to Fort William and we walked happily along the pavement as the sun beat down with increasing ferocity. Our mood had changed for the better now that the East Highland Way was almost behind us. We kept an eye on the map, and when we approached the point which marked one hundred miles left to go we all cheered and shook hands. Ally cracked the first joke of the day, announcing, "It's all downhill from here on in, guys!"

Around an hour later we reached the start of the West Highland Way. The van sitting in the car park was a welcome sight. All of the doors were open to try and encourage what little breeze there was to blow through. Food and drink was all set up on a table under a tree, which gave it some shade. Stevie came hobbling over with a great big grin on his face, lifting all our spirits instantly. "I've got all your stuff laid out," he said excitedly. Frank, Ally, and I threw ourselves down on the grass beside the table and Stevie instantly started presenting us with a choice of food and drink. I looked over at Jimmy and nodded towards Stevie. "He'll be okay," he said, and knowing Jimmy, I believed him. Stevie told us that he had been getting worried about us and had said to Jimmy, "Something's wrong

– they're late." Jimmy had replied calmly, "I was like that the first day, you'll get used to it."

We were happily tucking into our food when Ally turned to Stevie and said, "Jeeves, fetch me water!" We all laughed and started to give Jeeves our orders. Normal service had resumed with Stevie still very much part of the team, just in a slightly different role. We all posed for photos at the West Highland Way marker. For a bit of a laugh, and as a dig at Frank (him being a Dundee supporter), I pulled a shemagh (an Arab style scarf) out of my bag. The joke being that I'm a Dundee United supporter and therefore known as an Arab. Frank was much distressed at the sight and refused to have his photo taken with me, which was just the reaction I was looking for. Of course we made him take a team photo anyway, much to his disgust.

The Speyside Way felt like a distant memory to us now, and the East Highland Way was done and dusted. Now we had the ninety-five miles of the West Highland Way in front of us, with some of the most breathtaking scenery in the world to help us ease the pain and fatigue. We wouldn't need any more maps or guide books since we were now on familiar territory. It's funny how things can change. We started the day with heavy hearts, and now, due to Stevie's renewed enthusiasm; the fact that we had less than a hundred miles to go; having the privilege of walking the West Highland Way once more; and the fact that we were all ripping the piss out of each other again meant that we were in a buoyant mood. We all shook hands and bid our farewells, knowing that we would meet up again in Kinlochleven at the end of the day. We set off on the West Highland Way with a spring in our step, eager to finish the day on a high.

We passed through Glen Nevis, the massive bulk of Ben Nevis on our left, then turned right, up a steep section of path that lead through some trees which thankfully gave us some respite from the blistering sun. My shemagh was originally just a joke, but it turned out to be just the thing to keep the sun off my sparsely covered head and bare neck. Since the West Highland Way is a major tourist attraction, we knew that the next part of the journey would not be as secluded as we had been used to so far. We all took a guess at how many people we would see before reaching Kinlochleven. Frank guessed the highest with sixty-four, a number which was soon surpassed. We found time to talk to a few and to offer encouragement to those who looked like they were on their last legs. "Not far now, keep it going, well done!" we would say as we applauded them. Some would stop to chat and ask if we were walking the route back to front. Most people walk south to north, so we were walking against the flow. We would just say yes, since we didn't want to belittle their achievement. Mind you, they must have walked away saying "Don't fancy their chances if they are in that state at the beginning of the walk." We eventually reached the stage that we weren't talking to the other walkers, or even to each other for that matter. The day had been so mentally and physically draining that we were now just focused on getting into Kinlochleven. Sometimes we would break into a jog to give our other muscles a rest, but after a while it was obvious that we were just shifting the pain about. After two hours walking along the old military road we got to the point where we could look out over to the beautiful Pap of Glencoe and down onto the very picturesque Kinlochleven, a thousand feet below.

We started on the descent towards it, down a very steep downhill section. I was in agony – shin splint hell it was – and I had to keep stopping when the pain got too much. Frank found it easier and less painful to charge down the hill as fast as possible, and under normal circumstances I would have done the same. Ally was struggling too, so when we finally got to the bottom it was such a relief for everyone. We took five minutes rest before walking the final mile to the Blackwater Hostel, our home for the night. When we arrived Jimmy was sitting on a bench in the porch and Frank was already in the shower. Stevie was sitting with Jimmy, but when he saw us he came hobbling over, trying to speak but laughing so hard that he couldn't get the words out. Ally and I started to laugh with him, we had no idea what we were laughing at, but clearly something was funny. Eventually, still gasping for breath, Stevie managed to share the joke. "W-we h-have a p-p-poorly German," he stammered out eventually, before instantly doubling up laughing again. Even though Ally and I didn't get the joke, we were still laughing uncontrollably along with Stevie's very infectious laugh. Eventually he managed to calm down and tell us that when they got into the room they woke up a guy who was lying in one of the bottom bunks. Stevie had nodded to him and said hello. In a heavy accent, the guy had responded, "I am German and I am very poorly." According to Jimmy, Stevie had been a wreck ever since. Although he did eventually calm down, I wouldn't have put money on him not having wet himself beforehand.

The room was nothing special, but it wasn't bad. To the right of the door there were two sets of bunk beds with a passageway between them and a window on the wall. The left side of the room was basically identical, except there was no window. Directly in front of the door was another one which led to a toilet and shower. There wasn't enough room for us to store all of our bags and boxes so I put my stuff on the landing outside. We all went for showers, I was last, as usual. When I came out the first thing I saw was Ally rolling around on the bottom bunk to my far left. His face was bright purple, teeth were clenched tight, and his hands were gripped tight to his foot. I instantly knew what the problem was: he was finally taking off those Compeed pads. "Having fun?" I asked.

His only response was, "Aaaah ya bastard!" This was directed at the Compeed pad in his hand, not me. I'm not even sure if he knew I was there. I went out to the landing to get ready and as I was sorting out my stuff I could hear Ally wrestling with the rest of the pads. There were cries of "Fuck!", "Aye-ya!" and a few more shouts of "Aah ya bastard!" And eventually, with a big gasping sigh, "Thank fuck!" before I heard him throw himself back on the bed. There was nothing but heavy breathing for a while and I peeked my head around the door to see him lying there, exhausted, sweat running down his face, looking like he had just given birth to twins.

When we were all finally ready we headed off to a nearby bar for food and a few well-earned pints. We chatted about our challenge and everyone who had gotten behind us so fantastically. These included people we hardly knew, and in some cases people who we didn't know at all. There were some who had heard about what we were doing and donated money on the Just Giving page. The people at Turnberry caravan site had given us hundreds, as had the employees of the Johnnie Walker bottling plant where Ally worked, even though they were going to be losing their jobs in a few months. My Aunt Cathy (Jimmy's sister and Ally and Stevie's mother) had made and sold jewellery. My friend Davie Dewar had arranged for me to meet a colleague of his, Jim, at Aberdeen airport to travel to London together on a Tartan Army trip. Even though I only met the guy once and hadn't seen him since, he took a sponsorship form from me, handed it around his workplace (Arjowiggins paper mill), and raised a good few hundred pounds. The guys at my and Frank's work had raised around a thousand pounds. The list was endless and we found it very humbling.

At one point during the night Jimmy said to me, "You should write a book about this adventure."

"And say what?" I replied, "Got up, had breakfast, walked, went to bed?" But once I'd had a proper think about it, I thought, why not!

We were all very tired so we didn't hang about long in the pub. When we got back to the hostel Stevie's German friend was nowhere to be seen. We all got into bed and started to drift off to sleep. Just before I had completely passed out Stevie said, "Poorly German" and burst into a fit of the giggles. Of course we all joined in. Not because we thought a German being unwell was anything to laugh about, but because Stevie's reaction to it was so funny. It must have looked like a mental home to an outsider. It's the only time in my life that I have fallen asleep mid-laugh.

Day 5 Kinlochleven to Tyndrum (28 miles)

I woke staring into the darkness, I could hear the rain slightly patting the window and could tell instantly it was dark and gloomy outside. I was drifting back to sleep when that irritating sound of the alarm going off startled me back into this world. I lay for a moment listening to the dawn chorus. BURRRRRUMPH!!!! A sound came from out of the dark, well, the darkness of Frank's arse. Then the sound of Ally's pleading voice saying, "Fuck's sake Frank. That better not smell of eggs." Ally can't look at an egg without throwing up. Everyone started moaning, groaning and complaining. We all moaned about the same painful things but in very different ways. Uncle Jimmy was already dressed and leaving for the kitchen. The same start to the day was now set in stone: painkillers and checking when we could get our next fix, applying plasters, Vaseline, and taking in food and fluids. When we arrived in the hostel kitchen Jimmy had toast and the coffee ready for us. All complaining stopped about sore anything and a quiet acceptance replaced all negativity. We knew what had to be done and it was time to shut up and get on with it.

We had found that once we stopped walking and sat down for any more than two or three minutes, when we started up again it would take anything up to half an hour for the pain to turn into a dull numbness that allowed us to walk something like normal. Usually our first steps after a rest were so painful that it made us look as if we were doing a very bad moonwalk. Therefore once we were on our feet we were very reluctant to sit down. So Frank, Ally, and I stood eating our breakfast and sipping our drinks, and chatting about the day ahead. Jeeves got his usual orders and we got our usual cheek back. We gathered our essentials, always doing a quick check: Paracetamol, Ibuprofen, water, food, plasters, etc. We said our farewells to Uncle Jimmy and Stevie, shook hands, and wished each other well.

We then made our way out of the cosiness of the hostel and into the damp gloom of the morning. Jimmy and Stevie would clean up, get everything into the van and make their way to Kings House: our first meeting point of the day 9 miles away. As soon as we came out of the hostel it was a left turn past the teeming torrent of the River Leven. The amount of rain through the night was evident as the river was running as if it was in spate, the water was dark and the noise of it rushing past us was deafening. Ally shouted, "Refreshing!" sarcastically through the noise as he looked at the raging torrent.

We started walking the endless climb up to the back top end of the Devil's Staircase, which wound like a tangled piece of rope endlessly upwards.

Although very beautiful, remote, and usually inspiring, this time we found it a slog. Our thighs and calve muscles were burning, but it did at least give me some relief from my shin splints. I mentioned this to Ally and his reply was predictable, "Sod your shins."

We spoke as we climbed about anything to keep our minds off of what we were doing. We spoke about family and friends, about our tartan army trips. Before we knew it we were at the top of the Devil's Staircase and looking down into Glen Coe and the A82. Frank appeared as if by magic beside us, and said, "It's all downhill from here." Meaning downhill to Kings House. I said to Ally and Frank, "You go ahead, shin splint hell for me."

They both nodded and made their descent. You may think that they should have waited for me but for them to hold back would have been as sore as for me to try to keep up. If you have never had shin splints it is like someone giving you a slight kick repeatedly from the bottom to the top of your shin. Certain ways you walk are worse than others. For me, downhill was a nightmare.

I stumbled, fumbled, and fell but somehow got to the bottom next to the A82, just facing the stunning Buachaille Etive Mor, a majestic group of three mountains which I have been lucky enough to climb a couple of times, with both Ally and Frank being in that climbing party. Ally and Frank were getting waterproof clothes and other bits and pieces sorted when I caught up with them. Ally said, "That's the worst of it for you now."

Frank, being in no mood for hanging about, just said, "Right then."

'Right then' in Frank talk means 'I've had enough of this dawdling, let's get going'. We marched along quite happily, not really saying much and making quite good progress. Every now and then we would say hello to the people who were walking the West Highland Way as they passed. We were about a mile from the meet point when this American couple stopped and asked, "Is this the West Highland Way"

I replied, "Yes." Ally and Frank just kept walking.

They then asked, "Is this Glen Coe?"

I replied, "Yes."

They then asked, "Where is the Glen Coe visitor's centre?"

I replied, "The other end of Glen Coe, about 15 miles away." Sensing a chance for a bit of fun I asked, "Is it the Glen Coe Massacre you're interested in?"

Wide eyed they both in unison said, "Yes."

I tried to look as serious as possible, asking quietly, "You're not Campbells are you"?

"No, we're Nisbits," they replied excitedly.

"Just as bad," I snapped angrily.

I was joking but they obviously thought I was serious by the shocked look on their faces. I spent the next 10 minutes trying to make light of things and explain about the Campbell and MacDonald thing. However I think I terrified them and they just wanted to be as far away from me as possible

I caught up with Ally and Frank at the King's House. King's House is a big white hotel/inn just off the main A82 road, it's popular with walkers walking the West Highland Way and also with skiers as it is just next to the ski slopes of Glen Coe. It also has a herd of wild deer visiting them every now and then, they usually get a free meal from the staff when they show up. As I arrived Jimmy was filming our arrival with a camcorder, Stevie had our gear and food prepared for us. I was telling them about my encounter with the American couple and how they just did not appreciate my sense of humour. This has happened to me before and since.

We were soon fed and watered and made our way to the next meet point, Inveroran, which was 10 miles from Kings House. If the descent from the Devil's Staircase was shin splint hell for me, for all of us the next 3 miles was going to be sore feet horror, although we didn't know that at the time. We crossed the A82 towards the Glen Coe Ski centre, then after the ski centre car park we climbed up a very rocky path with loads of little sharp stones that pushed against the soles of our shoes, which in turn pushed against our bruised and blistered feet. Ally was the first victim, he obviously stood on a very sharp rock, "AH! FUCK, FUCK, FUCK!" He shouted out in pain.

Frank and I turned towards Ally to see what was wrong, we looked at each other, then burst out laughing. Almost instantly I took a step forward and felt the pain shoot through my foot as the sharp hard rock pressed against the sole of my right foot, "AH FUR FUCK SAKE!" I shouted.

For the next hour the three of us must have looked like a Tourette's syndrome walking group, with shouts of, "FUCK!"

"BASTARD!"

"BASTARD! BASTARD! BASTARD!"

"FUCK THIS SHIT!"

"FUCKING FUCK PIG BASTARD!" and so on, every time we stood on a sharp rock or stone, which was often. We eventually got past that section after about an hour and stood for a minute to get our composure back. We didn't say too much at first, we just looked at each other with a look of relief. Then Ally said, "That was fun will we go back and do it again?" We all gave a nervous laugh and in unison started to look through our bags for our selection of painkillers, not even caring if it was in our time slot. The next section was across Rannoch Moor, which is a bleak open area with an old cobbled military road for us to walk on. This was not good for our feet either but for most of it we could walk to the side of it and avoid the cobbles.

For a large part of the day we were walking in drizzly rain but now the heavens had opened and it was raining heavily. We just put our heads down and marched on and actually made really good time, all things considered. The military road ended and a normal minor road took its place. This allowed the three of us to up the pace considerably and we were walking quicker than we had from the first day. We were at Inveroran so quickly that, for the first time, Uncle Jimmy and Stevie were not ready for us.

Ally's workmate Ian had arranged to meet us at Inveroran. Ian is a keen photographer and he was traveling all the way up from Ayrshire to lend his support and take some photos of us. Inveroran has nothing in it apart from a hotel with a small cafe attached. It was really strange having Ian there inside our wee bubble and as strange as it sounds it was quite unsettling for me. This had nothing to do with Ian himself. I liked him instantly, I have been in his company many times since and really get on well with him. I'm not quite sure why it was unsettling, I think maybe because the only people that could possibly understand what we were going through was the five of us.

As it was raining so heavily we had our lunch in the cafe. It turned out to be quite a morale booster, as did Ian joining our bubble, he also continually ripped the piss out of Ally which we all loved. We put on dry clothes, had hot food and drink, and with our spirits lifted we said our thanks and farewells to Ian. The rain had all but stopped so we spoke to Stevie and Jimmy about what the plan would be when we got to Tyndrum, our finishing point for the day, 9 miles away. Our new found vigour lasted as long as our first steps as the pain was quite intense until the numb effect took over. From the cafe it was almost straight up and over a hill of about 700ft, under normal circumstances it wouldn't have been a problem but at this stage of the game it was tough going. To be honest for me more than

Frank and Ally, Frank was his usual self, half man-half machine. Ally seem to struggle a bit early on but had recovered quite quickly and seemed to be in reasonably good shape. We got up to the top of the hill and I went to get some water out of my bum bag. It wasn't there. Then I remembered that I hung it over the chair in the cafe. I thought about going to get it for a split second as my camera, phone etc. was in it. I said to Frank and Ally quietly in an 'I give up' kind of way, "I left my fucking bag in the cafe".

Ally replied, "Was your phone and everything in it?"

"Aye."

Frank said with a very wry smile, "Good luck. See you in Tyndrum." Then he said, "Uncle Jimmy will go back for it."

"Good call," I said with relief.

So we headed down the hill towards Bridge of Orchy trying to get hold of Uncle Jimmy on the phone, and of course we couldn't get a signal. We got down to Bridge of Orchy railway station, crossed the tracks, and Ally said, "Medication time," with a laugh.

I want for my bag and of course no bag meant no pain killers. Ally took out the usual mix of pain killers and anti-inflammatory tablets, put out his arm to hand me them and when I was about to take them from his hand he closed hand and said, "Fifty quid."

I said, "No problem, but you'll need to take it out your mouth because I'll stick so far up your arse that's the only way you'll get access to it."

Of course this was all said tongue and cheek. Ally opened his hand so I could get my fix. I saw Frank gazing up at the two mountains in front of us as the clouds started to lift and the sun started to shine. I said to him in a whisper, "I'm surprised you're not rocking back and forward."

Frank laughed and said, "Brrrrr!" While mockingly shivering.

To explain this to the reader I'm going to have to take you back about two years. Frank, myself, and our friend Davie Dewar were claiming these two mountains. We made our way between the two mountains until we reached the saddle where we had a choice of going left or right to reach the summit of one the peaks, then come back to the saddle, go the opposite way and climb the other summit. Davie has a similar stocky build to me, about five foot seven, he is quite dark in hair and skin. Davie has a wicked sense of humour and one of these people that when he talks everyone stops to listen. When we got to the saddle it was a very warm spring day with not a cloud in the sky and Davie thought it a good idea to leave our rucksacks at the saddle with food, clothing and waterproofs as it was only about an hour to the summit. Davie disputes that it was his idea to leave the rucksacks to this day. About 10 minutes from the first summit Davie tapped me on the shoulder, pointed in the opposite direction from where we were heading and said matter-of-factly, "That doesn't look good."

I knew instantly what he meant. There was a very large dark angry cloud about 5 miles wide. The bottom of it was almost hitting the Glen floor three thousand feet below us, and the top of the cloud went up to heaven somewhere. I said to Davie, "That monster's coming after us, isn't it?"

Davie never said a word and just nodded slowly. I shouted at Frank who was just ahead of us, "Check that monster!"

Frank looked and said simply, "Let's summit."

We very quickly got to the summit and immediately started our descent towards the approaching storm hoping to make the saddle and our rucksacks to get our winter clothes and waterproofs before the storm reached us. The three of us were stupid. Stupid to leave our gear at the saddle, stupid not turn back as soon as we saw the approaching storm, and stupid to not take the minimum essentials with us from our rucksacks. We are Scottish, we know how the weather can change in the mountains, this has happened to all of us before, but we have always had our kit with us. We were twenty minutes from the summit when the edge of storm hit us. The temperature dropped from around eighteen to just above freezing in an instant, the wind was buffeting but not a real problem, and the visibility was okay.

When the gradient wasn't too bad we ran and when steep we slowed it down and took deliberate cautious steps as the wind had strengthened and was throwing us off balance. When we were about half an hour from the saddle the wind picked up even stronger, it got darker, and the hail started. The wind driven hail was hitting us head on, with great force. We could barely walk without getting blown off our feet, and the temperatures had dropped to well below freezing. Then out of the blue I had to make a call of nature. As the guys reading this will know, and the ladies may think they know, the male reproductive organ does not like cold. In particular it does not like freezing cold wet hands trying to grab it. Therefore, as soon as I tried to get hold of it, it looked like a cockle recoiling into its shell, albeit a hairy shell. I had to go, there was nothing else I could do, so I dropped my shorts and pants to my ankles and let nature take its course, hands free if you like, with my back to the wind. The wind carried my wee for miles. Davie shouted, which I could barely make out over the sound of the gale-force wind, "No fucking way would I bring that out in this." The three of us eventually got to our rucksacks and crouched down behind a large rock the size of a small car to protect us as best we could against the elements. Frank, being diabetic, has to look after his extremities so we helped him put his gloves on as he just could not make his hand work due to the cold.

Needless to say we did not climb the other mountain that day and instead we had made our way back, now with full winter clothes on, to where we were currently standing. We continued along the soft sand-type foot path from Bride of Orchy to Tyndrum, which was as comfortable on our feet as it could be. We started to relax as we walked. The sun was drying us off nicely and steam was coming off us as we walked. We had a bit of a laugh at how we must have looked to the West Highland Way-ers as they passed us. I think it's fair to say we walked into the campsite in Tyndrum looking like three tramps, but with a swagger. Uncle Jimmy and Stevie were there to greet us, we shook hands and gave man hugs, and there was something about us now as a group that wasn't there at the start. We had come a long way in terms of how we communicated and interacted with each other. We helped and encouraged each other, and kicked each other in the arse when it was needed. Doing something like this you are laid bare, your true personality comes out, there is no mask to hide behind, you learn a lot about yourself and each other and a natural bond develops which can last a lifetime.

The tent was up and our gear laid out for us. It was just a matter getting showered and going for food. After my shower Jimmy took me to get the bum bag I left in the cafe. It took about twenty minutes to get there. As soon as the van stopped I got out and made my way to the table where we had been sitting and, to my surprise, the bag was exactly where I had left it. There was no one in the cafe so I just took it and left. I don't know if they knew it was there and just expected me to come back for it, or if they just didn't notice it.

Twenty minutes later we were back at Tyndrum. Our allocated space was a gravel pitch with grass all round, with a couple of logs placed end to end at the end of the pitch, which I assume was to stop the cars driving onto the grass. We had a table set up with a kettle, wine, beer and some nibbles. I got out of the van and Frank handed me some red wine in a plastic tumbler. He raised his glass and said warmly, "Cheers, two to go"

I raised my tumbler and said, "Slàinte." Stevie raised his glass and never said a word, just nodded his approval. Ally was in the tent mumbling about something and came out of the tent and said, "Aye cheers." then sat down on the log as did my Uncle Jimmy. I went to the toilet and came back to them all laughing hysterically. Jimmy had rolled off the log and ended up flat on his back, legs and arms up in the air, doing the dying fly. He could not get up for laughing and the more he laughed the more they did. They were all in real danger of wetting themselves till they noticed Jimmy was laughing so hard he was in some discomfort. They got him to his feet all out of breath, and that's when I came in. For the first time we had some time to relax, we were ready and it was only eight o'clock. The mood was good and we walked along to the bar near the Green Welly shop. Why this is called the Green Welly Shop I'll never know, it sells everything but green wellies.

We had a relaxing meal, chatted and laughed, we told Stevie and Jimmy about how our day went, they told us about some funny moments they had as we walked back to the tent. We brushed our teeth, had some water and were in our sleeping bags in no time. We were drifting off to sleep when Stevie started giggling like a school girl. "What are you laughing at?" Ally asked, laughing along.

Stevie just managed to get out through his laugh, "Poorly German."

The five of us were rolling about, kicking and screaming, gasping for breath as we all ended up in hysterics. In itself it wasn't funny but Stevie's reaction to it was so, so funny. The laughter died down and there was silence. I lay looking up at the tent roof as the light faded slowly and my consciousness faded with it.

Day 6 Tyndrum to Balmaha (33 miles)

This day started off slightly differently from the rest: for the first time, I had to be wakened. I felt Frank giving me a gentle kick. He looked down at me and said calmly, "You alright mate?"

I looked up at him, trying to bring him into focus, and nodded as I slowly sat up. I felt like shit. A few days earlier I had noticed one of my gums feeling puffy and tender, and it had now turned into a full-blown, very painful, abscess. I was cold and shivery. As I stood up, I almost fell, and would have gone straight back down again if Frank hadn't grabbed me. He asked me again, a little less calmly this time, "You alright?"

I just put my forehead on his shoulder and steadied myself, nodding that I was okay. I tried to sit down, but more slumped on top of my sleeping bag, as Frank took my weight to make my landing a bit gentler. He handed me a bottle of water and as I drank it I felt myself coming to almost instantly. "Thanks, big man," I said more confidently as I felt myself coming back to life again. I have a real problem in drinking all of my water. It's not that I don't drink, it's just I feel the need to keep some, which sometimes leaves me dehydrated.

I went through usual routine: painkillers, Vaseline, plasters, put my clothes on, and made my way out of the tent into the bright sunshine – and midgie hell. Everyone was in good spirits and looked ready to go. Stevie handed me coffee and a flapjack, "Cheers, Stevie," I whispered as I sat down on the log next to Ally, who had a midgie net over his head, as did Uncle Jimmy. I just wrapped my big scarf round my head which helped keep the midgies away and allowed me to take in food and drink. It was a really nice morning. Not one of us moaned about anything, we had stopped listening to each other on that score and it didn't help anyway. Then came a major boost just at the perfect moment. I went over to Stevie and held out my cup and said, "Any more coffee?"

"Aye," he replied with a smile.

"'You alright?" I asked, wondering what he was smiling about.

"I'm going to walk tomorrow, I'm going to finish it with you."

My response was a muted, "Nice one," but inside I was on cloud 9. We started together, we'll finish together. That really gave me a boost. I was up for it now. It was just a matter of getting the 33 miles today finished and the last day would take care of itself. As we set off around 6:30am we shook hands with Stevie and Jimmy, wished each other luck, and started making our way to our first stop of the day: Inverarnan, 19 miles away. Just behind our tent was a small burn we crossed to take us onto the West Highland Way path. The path at this point is wide and flat and we made good progress as we continued along, winding our way through trees, and eventually climbing upwards high above Crianlarich, a small village that is a popular stopping point for walkers. I wasn't sure if Stevie made his intentions of walking the last day with us known to Frank and Ally so I didn't mention it even though I was bursting to talk about it. Then Ally said, "Stevie is going to walk the last day with us." Fantastic, we all knew, and that was much of our conversation for the first part of the walk. My mind was focused on Stevie, and the painkillers were helping. The three of us were gibbering like fishwives, no one was listening and everyone was talking, the time flew by. Before I knew it we were high above the A82 and the path was taking us down next to the road just before the very impressive Falls of Falloch. High above us was the Munro Ben More, which Ally, David Duff and I claimed on a very dank grey day just over a year ago.

We followed the path next to the road for about a mile, then had to crouch down under a small bridge which took us under the road and out into a path that lead to the Falls of Falloch. We walked along the river steadily descending and eating up the miles. Then up a gentle hill till Loch Lomond came into view for the first time. We all stopped and stared saying nothing. This was a moment for us all but Ally more so. This area was Ally's playground, he knew it like the back of his hand. For Frank and me it meant the end was near, for Ally it meant he was home and he knew every inch of the way back to Glasgow. We savoured the moment and took some photos. It was a warm sunny day and we strolled down hill to Beinglas Campsite where we were meeting Uncle Jimmy and Stevie.

When we arrived the food and drink was laid out and we were chatting away. We were going to be walking on the east side of Loch Lomond and the road was on the west which meant that Jimmy and Stevie would have to travel all the way down to the bottom of the Loch, and then make their way back up the other side till they reached Rowardennan where the road stopped: a 30 mile trip for them. As we were chatting this big burly man came up and said in a rage, "You can't stop and eat here, we have a shop that sells food."

Before we could reply, my Uncle Jimmy, who was approaching seventy at the time, turned on this guy and said with clenched fists, walking towards him with total aggression, "Your fucking shop's shut." I truly thought at that moment Jimmy was going to plant one on him and so did the man obviously because he backed away and said sheepishly, "Don't be long," and walked away. Jimmy turned calmly round and said, "More coffee anyone?" We just burst out laughing. The talk for the next five minutes was about what a dick that guy was. It was also one of the few times I ever heard Uncle Jimmy swear.

We all knew that the next seven miles was going to be tough. Inverarnan to Inversnaid is the most energy sapping seven miles of the West Highland Way. It's pretty much a cliff along the shores of the Loch with a path along the edge. There are obstacles such as fallen trees, ladders, enormous boulders, awkward ups to climb, and awkward downs for about six of the seven miles. This section finishes a lot of people walking the Way when they get to this part on their second or third day at the 30 mile point from the start of the walk. At this point, we were taking this section on after over two hundred miles. However, we also knew what to expect and we just wanted it done. From Beinglas Campsite it's a steady climb up for about half an hour then an easy walk down through trees to the very start of the north end of the Loch. From here, it's boulder hopping till you get onto the cliff path. As you go along you sometimes have the water about three feet below you and at others it about sixty feet below you. It's really tough going and we had a return of the Tourette's Walking Group again with shouts of, "FUCK!"

"BASTARD!"

"AYAA FUCKING FUCKER!"

"ARSEHOLE!"

"FUCK, FUCK, FUCK!"

As we fell, bashed our shins, and stood awkwardly on sharp bits of rock.

At the end of this hell on a path we came to the very tranquil setting of the Inversnaid hotel with seats and chairs outside. We sat there for half an hour having a beer looking over the Loch and the surrounding hills and mountains. We chatted about nothing in particular, just three men chewing the fat like we had just sat down in any normal situation.

The first time Frank and I walked the West Highland Way, we did it in two and a half days, carrying everything with us. Inversnaid was our first stop. We stayed in the Bunkhouse high above the hotel we were sitting in now. We had gotten in much later than expected and they had put the hot tub on for us as we waited for them to make us food. Frank had a glass of red and I had a pint of Guinness. We had just lay there, letting the bubbles and swirling water take all our aches away. We both could have done with a hot tub this time, I can tell you!

The daydreaming about hot tubs was brought to an abrupt end and I was brought back into the present and the real world when Frank said, "Right then." We had to force ourselves, groaning as we lifted ourselves off of the seats and tried to get going again. We all struggled for the first 500 yards till we loosened up. We did eventually start to quicken the pace a bit and were making progress but I was really struggling. Apart from the pain in my feet, legs, and mouth, I was feeling ill. I tried everything. I forced down food and fluids hoping to give me energy and drive but nothing was helping. I was at the stage of it being one foot in front of the other and could not think of much more than the next step. We eventually got into Rowardennan where Jimmy and Stevie were waiting in the hotel beer garden. As a wee surprise, Jaqueline, my wee cousin and Jimmie's daughter, was there to lend her support. Sam, Jaqueline's son, was with her, as was their wee dog Grommet. Jaqueline is around five six with dark hair and the clearest, fairest skin, she's one of these annoying people who just don't age. It was good to have her there with Sam. It gave us all a boost, but none more than Uncle Jimmy. It was good for him to have his daughter and grandson there. He must have been like the rest of us and flagging, because he had put a lot into the last six days and you could see him wilting a little as well. Sam was about six foot tall and full of beans, with dark hair like his mum. Jimmy, quite rightly, was so proud of him.

Stevie was drinking wine, Jimmy was sitting down, and they were enjoying the views. Frank and Ally sat down as if to settle into the cosiness of the situation. I was thinking, "bad idea gents, we have seven miles still to go, the jobs not done." I deliberately made a point of not sitting down and said, "Let's just fill the water bottles and get going." Jackie, to her credit, went straight away and got the water for us and we were soon on our way again. The next part of the walk was probably hardest for me in the entire 6 days. I was really struggling and felt that if I stopped I wouldn't get going again and the challenge would be over. I would have failed and not completed the walk, and I was terrified. From the planning stage we all knew that there was a possibility that some or none of us would finish this challenge, no point in doing it otherwise. I knew that I had to keep going till Day Six was over. I trundled along, focusing on making funny wee shapes in my mind to create positivity, keeping the negative thoughts away. After what seemed like hours of fighting mentally and physically to keep going I heard Ally shout. I looked up and saw that he was pointing to a laminated sign on a tree saying, "WELL DONE RONNIE, ALLY, STEVIE, AND FRANK. YOU'RE ALMOST THERE!!! XXXX." This was courtesy of Marion and David. I don't think I said to my sis to this day, but she could not have placed that sign with those words at a better time or a better place. That sign was the positivity that we all needed and from nowhere I developed a spring in my step that got me into the camp. When I arrived Ally's Jackie was there along with our now expanding support. I was so relieved to get in I gave Jackie a big hug as soon as I saw her. I don't think that hug would have been the nicest for her as I must have smelled pretty bad. There was only time for a quick drink before we had to get showered and ready to get our food at the Oak Tree Inn before it closed. Although I was in a lot of pain and feeling quite ill, what I was about to witness had me laughing so hard that the tears were rolling down my cheeks. Stevie was practising walking for the next day with his size 8 feet in Franks size 12 shoes to give his sore feet a bit more room. Stevie, not being used to the extra inches, was walking like a circus clown. He was just missing the curly wig, big red nose and the makeup. We were all laughing and it was made funnier by Stevie not understanding what we were laughing at. That set the mood for the evening and the extra company of Jaqueline, Sam, and Jackie made it more like a celebration than the last supper. Frank handing me his flask of whiskey to ease my pain helped even more. We had a really enjoyable meal and chatted about normal things in a normal situation which was a breath of fresh air and took us out of our bubble. Seemingly people were constantly calling, texting and emailing asking how we were getting on and wanting to know as much detail as possible. It was really nice for us to know that we captured the imagination of so many people. As we left the bar we bid our farewell to Jackie as she headed back to Glasgow. We all made kissing noises like school boys as Ally said his fond farewells to Jackie. Jaqueline and Sam were staying in a nearby hotel so we bid them good night and would see the on our first stop the next day.

With all the painkillers, whisky and beer I was in a state of quiet acceptance as I got into my sleeping bag and just lay there as everyone got into theirs. Frank was lying face down with his chin on his hands settling down for the night. I was just drifting off sleep when I heard a 'clunk' sound. Ally said, "OH FUCK!" followed by another 'clunk', then Frank shouted out in pain and his face twisted in agony. This was one of the few occasions I had seen Frank show how much in pain he was in. It took me a second or two to work out what had happened but I suddenly realised that Ally had hit his head off the lamp, knocking it off its hook, where it then fell straight onto Frank's raw, open wound of a heel. Ally was full of apologies, Stevie was biting his pillow trying and failing miserably not to laugh out loud. After all the noise and shouting died down I fell into a deep sleep. My last thought was, 'Tomorrow is the last day.'

Day 7 Balmaha to Milngavie (21 miles)

I opened my eyes and stared at the roof of the tent. I could hear Uncle Jimmy rumbling about looking for things and slowly everyone said, "Morning." one by one as they came to. There was a strange shriek of what I took to be an animal noise outside the tent on the Loch shore. We all in unison said, "What the fuck was that?" Frank knows about such things, being brought up on a farm, and said, as if we all should have known, "It's an oyster catcher."

Straight away, Ally replied in his monotone voice, "Blessed are the oyster catchers, for if it was not for the oyster catchers the world would be overrun with oysters."

We all burst out laughing uncontrollably, there were tears, slobbers and snotters everywhere as we rolled about kicking and screaming for breath. It may have been one of those 'you had to be there' moments, but at that time, at that place, and under those circumstances it was one of the funniest moments I have ever had. We still talk and laugh about it every time we are together.

We went through our usual routine, but we all had mixed emotions, knowing that this was the last time we would do all of this. The most overwhelming thought was 'thank fuck' though. Uncle Jimmy made us breakfast for the last time. Stevie was dressed and ready to join us, "Jeeves is dead long live Stevie," Frank said as we all raised our cups in salute. It was quite a pleasant breakfast, we chatted away as Uncle Jimmy filmed us. We laughed and joked till it was time to go, and we knew it was time to go because Frank said his usual, "RIGHT THEN!"

We put everything back in the van for the last time and said our farewells to Jimmy, leaving him on his own for the first time since Fort William. We made our way towards Balmaha and our only real obstacle of the day, Conic hill. As we made our ascent I said "STOP!" Everyone did just that.

I said in a whisper, "Did you hear that?"

Stevie whispered back, "What?"

I replied, "Uncle Jimmy singing and dancing that you're not there to annoy him."

Everyone groaned. "Ok that went down like a lead balloon," I thought.

As we reached the summit we all stopped to look at the view of Loch Lomond and the surrounding mountains, a view we have seen many times, however because of the light, weather, and seasons it never looks the same twice. It's one of the best views for the least effort you will ever get in Scotland. We took our last views of Loch Lomond and then made our way along the 8 miles to Drymen where we were meeting Uncle Jimmy, Jaqueline, and Sam. As we descended we stopped from time to time to speak to the West Highland Way goers. This, for most of them, was their first or second day. They were all fresh and enthusiastic. The four of us looked like bags of shite, and we drew some funny looks, especially Stevie hobbling along in his oversize trainers. Stevie and Frank were a little behind Ally and I. We were chatting away when we heard a very prominent Irish male accent say, "Fucking tell me you're not walking the Way in reverse!"

Ally said, "Aye we are."

The Irish man laughed and said, "Feck that! I'm heading back, I'm fucked if I'm ending up in that state." The three of us burst out laughing and Ally said, "We've done a wee bit more than that so don't worry." He was explaining what we were doing and why when we were interrupted by an American female voice saying, "Are you Scottish?" The three of us turned round to this very attractive girl of around twenty three. When I say attractive I'm talking 11 out of 10 attractive, drop dead gorgeous, stunningly beautiful, well you get the picture. We dropped our new Irish friend like a hot stone when he was in mid-sentence. Ally and I replied in unison in our most exaggerated Scottish accent, "Aye!"

I took it a bit further, repeating, "Aye, we urrr, lassie." The look that Ally gave me was meant to turn me to stone I'm sure. Our new found Irish friend didn't say a word, he just walked away. I would like to think he understood.

The American beauty asked, "Is it true about these goats?" I was fucked, we were on Ally's specialist subject. Ally was holding court with this girl and she was hanging on his every word. I just stood with my mouth open, looking as if I had had a lobotomy. As Ally and the beauty were chatting this man with dark hair, tanned skin, and a Colgate smile came over and said, "Hi," also with an American accent. "Boo," I thought, "her boyfriend." The American beauty said, "Oh, this is my brother." She did tell us his name but I can't remember it, when she said "brother" I thought "Hooray". So we went back into Ally holding court with both of them, and me standing there, mouth open, watching the lovely view, which had nothing to do with scenery. After far too short a time the Americans were saying goodbye, and as they walked away both me and Ally spoke of how much we enjoyed the young Americans lady's company and what a delight she was. I would like to say there was never a "CORRRR" uttered but my nose is big enough as it is.

When Frank and Stevie caught up with us we both asked in unison, "Did you see the big honey?"

"Don't think so," they replied.

"What'd she look like?" Frank asked.

Ally said, "If you're asking that you never seen her."

That was pretty much the end of that wee bit of excitement. We were coming up to Drymen and we were all looking forward to some hot fluids and some food. For June it was very cold and the drizzle was soaking us to the bone. We were in high spirits as we reached Uncle Jimmy, Jaqueline, and Sam. Stevie and Frank were again a few minutes behind us. As Stevie took his first steps on the tarmac we all turned round because when his feet hit road the extra four inches of trainer made a loud slapping noise. It sounded like a frogman walking behind us. We chatted away and I noticed that Jimmy for the first time in days had allowed himself to relax completely. Throughout the week, considering what we were doing, there were many light, funny moments and Uncle Jimmy, like the rest of us, had enjoyed those moments. I said we were a group in a bubble, but within that bubble Frank, Ally, Stevie, and I all went into our own wee bubbles from time to time. Looking at Uncle Jimmy, shoulders down, laughing like a school boy with the rest of us, I realised he couldn't do that, he couldn't go into his own wee bubble. There were so many times Jimmy was very concerned about us, individually, and as a group. He was up before us, there to greet us at the end of every day, and at every stop in between. He didn't have that opportunity of sinking into a bubble and worrying about himself. Now for him his job was pretty much done and you could feel and sense the relief in him.

We didn't hang about long in Drymen as our next stop and lunch was at the Beech Tree inn just an hour away, the rain was belting down in sheets so we wanted to get moving and we were getting wetter by the second. Our waterproof clothing had long stopped working so it was head down and get going. We reached the Beech Tree Inn before Jimmy was ready so we had go back out into the rain so Jimmy could film us as if we had just arrived. With Jimmy staying under the shelter of the inn, I may add.

It was so good to get in from the rain and the four of us went straight to the van to get our boxes and dry clothes. I don't think any of us had clean clothes left and we weren't caring anyway. The Inn had an outside wooden canopy and we just undressed there, and dried ourselves best we could. I put a towel round my waist, dropped my soaking wet pants to the floor, dried everything under the towel, and put a pair of fresh, clean pants on. Don't underestimate what a morale booster it is to have a dry cosy bottom and dangly bits. Then it was on with a dry fleece, and a pair of dry leggings. There was no way at that moment with all that dry cosiness was I going to put my feet into soaking wet trainers so I walked bare foot to the door of the bar, leaned against the wall and dried one foot, then the other. I put my towel on the floor and put one cosy dry sock on. BLISS. I then put a warm, sock-clad, foot into the door of the pub. Then put my other warm cosy sock on. BLISS. I then put my other foot into the pub, bent down picked up the towel which I threw to the side just outside the door. I turned round and walked through a second set of doors and out of the dark, wet, cold gloom and into the cosy, warm, dryness of the pub. That moment was almost spiritual.

I went into the toilet where Frank had his hands under hot running water, trying to get heat into them. We all gathered and sat at a table away from the main bar, a pint of Guinness was put in front of me and was emptied in less than five minutes. Hot soup, bread, chips, and another pint of Guinness were put down in front of me, which I savoured. My morale was truly boosted, we had 8 miles left to go, and the heavy rain had eased considerably. We were all high: pains, illness, and fatigue were forgotten. The food and drink was all finished. It was time to go, time to finish this challenge. We made our way out of the bar. The rain had stopped although it was still overcast. We walked Uncle Jimmy to the van where he said with his voice full of emotion, "Well done boys, see you at the finish."

One by one we shook Jimmy's hand warmly and thanked him for getting us to the end. Jimmy drove off and we all watched the van disappear as he went off into the distance. Our spirits were high, knowing that in a few hours we would be at the end. We walked on, laughing and joking as if we were just heading out for a stroll to the pub on a hot summer's day. We could now talk about it because it was just about to happen: warm cosy beds, hot baths, long lies, watching TV. Normal life was about to resume. Even better for me, I was away to Portugal for a week's holiday. This I rubbed in with great delight! We were approaching Mugdock Park, all in good spirits, when I felt this burning feeling in my stomach, then a wee bit of a rumbling in the bottom of my tummy. I threw everything at Ally: bag, jacket, water, phone and said as I was rushing away, "I'll catch up!" Ally, Frank and Stevie were looking at me in bemusement. I hid myself as best I could, dropped my pants, assumed the sitting position and let the burning contents of my bowels empty with some force and plenty of noise. I could hear the guys piss themselves laughing as the penny dropped. I don't want to go into too much detail but it wasn't good. Over the course of about an hour I went another six or seven times. All the way to the finish was the same, stopping to go through same motion, if you'll pardon the pun. This all to the delight of Ally, Frank and Stevie.

The phones were going with so many well-wishers congratulating us, family and friends waiting at the finish to greet us asking how long we would be. We got to around half a mile from the finish and stopped to take a minute out for ourselves, shaking hands, big man hugs, thanking each other and congratulating each other. Someone brought out a very nice whisky, I think it was Ally. So we raised a glass to the five of us, all the people who supported us, and donated cash for action for children. It was time to finish, a very funny feeling and a huge range of emotions. We walked the last fifteen minutes not saying too much at all. We turned the corner just before the start of the West Highland Way where our welcoming committee was standing to meet us. We finished the big walk at around 1:30pm, six and a half days after we started and it was at that point we walked out of our bubble and into the real world again.

Of course the first person we wanted to see was Uncle Jimmy. We surrounded him, and I think he was equally as pleased to see us. My wife Alison was there, as was Marion my big sis, David her better half, Frank's wife Carol, Ally's partner Jackie, Jaqueline, and Sam. My aunt Cathy (Stevie and Ally's mum) was there with her husband Allan, Jackie's mum and dad and of course Grommet. There was champagne, poppers, whisky, banners. You could see passers-by thinking 'What a lot of fuss for a wee walk!!'

There were photos being taken with the five us next to a big Action for Children banner. Eventually, it was time to go and leave each other for the first time in a very intensive week. We had a reception and meal booked that night with all our family and friends. So we had to get home and sorted for that.

Alison, Marion, David, and I made our way to Marion's car. I sat in the back seat and as soon as the car started to move I burst into tears and sobbed uncontrollably. Where that wave of emotion came from I have no idea, and the more I tried to pull myself together the worse I got. I did eventually stop and was more than a little embarrassed. When we got to Marion's house where we were staying I could feel that sensation of allowing everything to go, and it's a smashing feeling. When you do these challenges as a younger man your body has a better recovery time at the end of each day and you don't need to fight quite as hard with your mind. Your body is saying, "No you can't." and you have to force your mind to tell the body,

"Yes you can." When, like Frank and I, you're 49 and 50, you have a much harder job telling your tired and sore body, "Yes you can." So I was in that lovely position where you can let your mind tell your body, "It's okay, it's over." Before I knew it I had a glass of whisky in my hand, a blanket was wrapped around me and my bruised, blistered, and swollen feet were in a hot foot bath. The last thing I remember as I feel into a very deep sleep was Marion saying how terrible we all looked, I don't think she knew I was not quite asleep yet. I just thought, "You should see it from the inside," as I sniggered to myself.

I was woke up to Alison saying, "Its six o'clock, I'll put the shower on. You need to get ready." I tried to bring everything into focus, Marion, David, Alison, Cathy, and Allan were all dressed up and looking a million dollars. I tried to focus, but was having difficulty, I don't know how I got there but I was suddenly sitting in the shower with the water pouring over me. I truly did not want to go to the reception but everyone had made the effort, all the people closest to us were going to be there so I had to turn up.

In the end it turned out to be a really good night. The banter was brilliant, the food good, and the drink was flowing. Among all the people there was my friend Caroline. I would have never have known at the time but a few years later she was going to become my girlfriend after Alison and I split up pretty much out of the blue. There was no big drama, after 26 years of marriage it ended.

The next day Carol drove Frank, Alison, and I back to Aberdeen and again it's a wee bit of a blur. The first thing I can really remember clearly is waking up in my bed in the early hours of Sunday morning feeling really bad. Aches and pains were okay and what you expect, but what I had was burning: a horrible burning in my foot. It felt as if boiling water was being poured over it. I also felt really ill in general.

I woke Alison and said, "You need to take me to hospital." The look on her face and the way she just started to get ready told me that I didn't look so good. It was around 5am and the Aberdeen A&E was full of drunk people from the night before with all sorts of injuries. I gave my details and was told to take a seat. Before I knew it I was talking to a doctor. He looked me over and said, "You have a really bad infection in your foot. The other one doesn't look good either. What have you been up to?"

I said, "I just finished a sponsored walk."

Then Alison said, with some force, "It wasn't a sponsored walk, it was 238 miles in 7 days. Complete madness."

I don't know who was more shocked, me or the doc. The doctor's attitude changed in an instant. He was shouting demands at people to get things and was attaching all sorts of things onto me and in me. I did not feel well but not bad enough for all this nonsense.

The doctor sat in front of me and said, "I need you to listen to me Ronnie, you have a really bad infection, your body has stopped taking care of the parts of your body that are not important and is looking after your vital organs. We're going to admit you." After that I only heard, "Blah, blah, blah."

I said, "I can't. I'm going to Portugal on Tuesday."

It was a wee case of the doc saying, "No you're not." And me saying, "Yes, I am." Till he eventually said, "Okay." and gave me an injection, a heap of tablets, and instructions on when and how to take them.

He then said, "Remember, no alcohol."

I said, "Of course." Even though I knew and he knew that was not going to happen.

Ten days later I came back from Portugal a new man.

Epilogue

Stevie

Before I tell you about Stevie I want to tell you that the first part of the book was written soon after the big walk and the second part had been started five years later.

Stevie was understandably disappointed that he had to pull out through injury. He had open wounds and blisters on every part of his feet, between his toes, on his toes, heels and soles. He also had one hell of a chapped arse. Thankfully I did not see this injury but by all accounts the two separate cheeks of his arse that had been rubbing together were red raw and also had open wounds. Not enough Vaseline, Stevie! He did eventually become aware of how much he achieved personally and what he help us to achieve as a group.

I've been on the edge and seen people there over the years and Stevie was certainly there on that last day of his walk. To be fair I think from his very first step that day he was in pain which just got worse and worse as that day went on. It truly was getting dangerous and I'm pleased that he called it before I did.

We have vowed to one day soon go back to Loch Laggan, AKA 'that fuckin' Loch' and walk its length.

Stevie went back to his wife and children in Sweden and he had a story to tell, which I'm sure he milked with great gusto. Unfortunately, Stevie and his wife split a few years later but, like me, he has been very lucky to meet a very nice girl and seems to be very happy I'm pleased to say

Ally

About half way through the walk Ally seemed to be struggling and, by his own admission, it was looking doubtful for him. From somewhere he managed to recover very quickly and I would say that he finished the challenge stronger than any of us. It may be that having had a decade less on this planet allowed him to recover quicker, who knows.

Ally eventually tied the knot with Jackie. In typical Ally style he did this in secret with only Jackie's mum and dad as witnesses. The day before the wedding Ally had said to his in-laws to be, "Jackie and I will treat you to breakfast tomorrow, wear something smart, as it's quite fancy"

So they took them to the registry office and said, "Before breakfast, we're just going to get married and you are our witnesses." They were so pleased and they all had a good day. Ally phoned everyone to tell them the news and everyone was pleased and wished them all the best and every happiness. All this happened on St Andrews Day, as Ally's a man that wakes every morning and thanks God he's Scottish.

Uncle Jimmy

Although the big walk was very challenging for him, and like the rest of us it took its toll, it turns out it was the right thing just at the right time for my Uncle Jimmy. My Uncle Jimmy was trying to re-adjust to life after losing his wife and our aunt.

My Uncle Jimmy was amongst men and as you may have guessed none of us are shrinking violets. Jimmy was in the middle of it, the slagging, the fun, the down times, and he gave as good as he got. We give my Uncle Jimmy a lot of respect, not just because of who he is but because of how he's been with us as long as all of us can remember. Frank instantly felt the same about Jimmy and they got on like a house on fire. For the whole seven days Uncle Jimmy did not have time to think of anything else but where to go, when to be there, and what needed to be done.

He came out the other end of the big walk with a different purpose and a fresh outlook I think. As well as being completely knackered.

When big Frank was asked after the walk, "Have you anything to say?" Frank raised his finger to the sky and sang, "There's only one Uncle Jimmy."

Frank

Frank finished the big walk strong. Like the rest of us, he had sore everything, and like the rest of us, he had looked a lot better. Unlike the rest of us, however, four days later Frank was running ten miles. Since the big walk Frank and Carol have become grandparents to two lovely granddaughters. And you should see him with them. He is complete and utter mush and I love seeing him like that.

Frank pulled back on the Ultra Marathons and went between running and cycling. He's always done both but started to take cycling a bit more seriously. So he got himself a racing bike and Carol bullied him into wearing a helmet. Mid-February Frank was cycling on a back country road near his home when a car overturned and hit him. His injuries were horrendous and it was touch and go whether he was going to survive. Frank's son Gary phoned me to tell me what had happened. It came out of the blue and I was in complete and utter shock. The next day was a Sunday and Ally drove me up to see Frank. As we got to the hospital Gary met us at the door. Carol, Frank's daughter Nicola, Gary's wife wee Carol, Nicola's soon to be husband Ian, and David and Leslie Wylie (friends of Frank's for as long as I have been, if not longer) were all there. As soon as we saw each other it was tears and hugs. Carol took us through to see Frank and warned us not to expect Frank as we know him. He was in a coma and had tubes helping him breathe and monitors. He was all puffed up with drips going in and out of him. I burst into tears!

On Tuesday the 21st of March I got a phone call, "How you doing mate?" the voice said and I knew that voice very well. Frank at home and on the road to recovery.

Acknowledgements

I have to say a big thanks to Liz Todd for going over what I have written and making it legible. She will have to go over this bit also and will be all glaikit. When I started to write this I asked my then friend Caroline Todd if she thought Liz (her daughter) would mind looking over what I had written. So I would write about a day and send it to Liz and she would send it back for my approval. I got up to day 4 and didn't write anymore as life got in the way. When Caroline and I started to go out together, Liz and I got to know each other better as well. Four years after the walk, Liz and her partner Muireann gave me a birthday present.

Liz and Muireann don't just give you a present they really think about what they give, it's always personal, and it is always a complete surprise. They told me they were sorry but my present would be late and a couple of weeks after my birthday they gave me my present which was the book you've just read, only just up until the end of day four. I had forgotten all about it and was in complete shock when I took off the wrapping paper to see just what you are seeing now. To say I was shocked and surprised just does not describe it. I can't describe it. I think I did my lobotomy thing again and just sat with my mouth open. Anyway it gave me the push to finish it. So thank you very much girls I doubt you will ever surpass that gift.

Printed in Great Britain
by Amazon